Aries

21 March – 20 April

First published in Great Britain 2010
by Harlequin Mills & Boon Limited,
Eton House, 18-24 Paradise Road, Richmond, Surrey TW9 1SR

ISBN: 978 0 263 87342 9

Typeset at Midland Typesetters Australia

Harlequin Mills & Boon policy is to use papers that are natural, renewable and recyclable products and made from wood grown in sustainable forests. The logging and manufacturing processes conform to the legal environmental regulations of the country of origin.

Printed and bound in Spain
by Litografia Rosés S.A., Barcelona

Dedicated to The Light of Intuition

Sri V. Krishnaswamy—mentor and friend

With thanks to Julie, Joram, Isaac and Janelle

About
Dadhichi

Dadhichi is one of Australia's foremost astrologers. He has the ability to draw from complex astrological theory to provide clear, easily understandable advice and insights for people who want to know what their futures might hold.

In the 27 years that Dadhichi has been practising astrology, face reading and other esoteric studies, he has conducted over 9,500 consultations. His clients include celebrities, political and diplomatic figures, and media and corporate identities from all over the world.

Dadhichi's unique blend of astrology and face reading helps people fulfil their true potential. His extensive experience in western astrology is complemented by his research into the theory and practice of eastern systems of astrology.

Dadhichi is a regular columnist for several Australian magazines. He often appears as a guest on leading Australian television and radio networks, where many of his political and worldwide forecasts have proved uncannily accurate.

His websites www.astrology.com.au, www.facereader.com, www.soulconnector.com and www.psychjuice.com attract hundreds of thousands of visitors each month, and offer a wide variety of features, helpful information and services.

Contents

Welcome from Dadhichi

Dear Friend,

Welcome to your astrological forecast for 2011! I've spent considerable time preparing these insights for you. My goal is to give you an overview of your sign and I hope you can use my simple suggestions to steer you in the right direction.

I am often asked by my clients to help them understand their true path and what they are supposed to be doing in life. This is a complex task; however, astrology can assist with finding some answers. In this book I attempt to reveal those unique character traits that define who you are. With a greater self-understanding, you can effectively begin *to live who you are* rather than wondering about *what you should do*. Identity is the key!

Knowing when the best opportunities in your life are likely to appear is the other benefit of astrology, based on planetary transits and forecasting. The latter part of the book deals with what is *likely* to happen on a yearly, monthly and daily basis. By coupling this section with the last chapter, an effective planner, you can conduct your business, relationships and personal affairs in ways that yield maximum benefits for you.

Along with your self-knowledge, there are two other key attitudes you must carry with you: *trust* and *courage*. Unless you're prepared to take a gamble in life, earnestly and fearlessly, you'll stay stuck in the same place, never really growing or progressing. At some point you have to take a step forward. When you synchronise yourself with the powerful talents found in your Sun sign, you'll begin to understand what your mission in life will be. This is the true purpose and use of astrology.

So I invite you to gear up for an exciting fifteen months! Don't shrink back from life, even if at times some of the forecasts seem a little daunting. Don't forget that humans are always at their best when the going gets tough. The difficult planetary transits are merely invitations to bring out the best in yourself, while the favourable planetary cycles are seasons for enjoying the benefits that karma has in store for you.

Remain positive, expect the best, and see the beauty in everyone and everything. Remember the words of a great teacher: 'The world is as you see it.' In other words, life will reflect back to you only what you are willing to see.

I trust the coming fifteen months will grant you wonderful success, health, love and happiness. May the light of the Sun, the Moon and all of the stars fill your heart with joy and satisfaction.

Your Astrologer,

Dadhichi Toth

The Aries Identity

What you see depends on what you're looking for.

—Anonymous

Aries: A Snapshot

Key Characteristics

Determined, fiery, executive skills, born leader, impulsive, headstrong, opinionated, loyal, physical, driven, ambitious

Compatible Star Signs

Leo, Sagittarius and Gemini

Key Life Phrase

I am

Life Goals

To be the best and be first; to be a leader rather than a follower

Platinum Assets

Enthusiasm, inspiration and fearlessness

Zodiac Totem

The Ram

Zodiac Symbol

♈

Zodiac Facts

First sign of the zodiac; movable, hot and dry

Element

Fire

Famous Arians

Russell Crowe, Celine Dion, Jackie Chan, Elle Macpherson, Ashley Judd, Sarah Jessica Parker, Steven Seagal, Conan O'Brien, David Letterman, Emma Thompson, Ewan McGregor, David Frost, Adolf Hitler, Dudley Moore, Heath Ledger

Aries: Your profile

Your zodiac birth sign of Aries represents new beginnings, the commencement of things, youth and exuberant energy, which is why Aries-born individuals are always so full of spirit and such high energy levels. You are a warm and endearing individual.

The fire sign under which you were born is creative and therefore you are creatively energised by this astrological element. You want creativity to be a part of your life, and because of this, you're not just a spectator but are totally involved in all of life's affairs.

You have incredible self-confidence, power and zeal. This also makes you very strong in your opinions and sometimes others might equate this with having an extremely large ego, which you probably wouldn't deny, would you now, Aries?

Speed is your middle name. You love living on the edge and want your life to be exciting. The Aries experience of life is actually quite thrilling. You hate boredom and want to spend your life with people who are equally as energetic as yourself.

One of the famous Aries traits is courage, and in the face of adversity, you're able to rise to the occasion, never shrinking or pulling back. Sometimes, however, you do tempt fate and may compromise your safety and personal security. You do tend to be reactive in situations, so there's a need to curb your hair-trigger temperament. Try not to provoke others and be a little more patient.

The Aries temperament is irritable, and because you want fast results, you sometimes compromise tolerance. One of your important goals in life is to nurture forbearance and be patient with others.

You are inspirational and aspire to be number one. You want to be the best and work well under adverse situations. Others look up to you. When people get to know you a little more intimately, they see that your insistent and sizzling exterior is only a part of your larger-than-life character. Behind your daring persona rests a warm and caring spirit.

Those who know you best will confirm that, although you do tend to have a big ego, you are most definitely a generous and loving individual whom they treasure as a friend. This is because you have the knack of making up for your imperfections by being so passionate and excited about everything you do.

You need to be in control of your situation and resent others pushing you around. But you must never take well-meaning advice as a challenge to you. Remember, Aries, you can always learn something from others, even if you don't at first see the sense or logic behind it.

You're capable of sharing your great ideas with people and should never shy away from teamwork. You can help those around you become better at what they do through your own leading example. Part of this example involves reaching for the sky and attempting goals that others would never dream of. This is definitely your specialty. You are an adventurer, an explorer; someone who hates treading the same old beaten path.

You aim for your goals and give 100 per cent of yourself in the process. Sometimes your style is a little tense and hard-nosed, but people who know you soon learn that if they want to be in the company of an Aries, they have to keep up with your pace. Your motto to them is: 'If you can't stand the heat in the kitchen, get out!'

Three classes of Aries

If you're an Aries born between the 21st and the 30th of March, Mars doubly rules and controls your destiny. You are full of fire and, on many occasions, brimstone, too. Power, vitality and high levels of energy mark you out from others. You need to get heavily involved with sports and other physical activities that will give you adequate outlets for your energy.

You are a great leader and often challenge the status quo because you believe that things can be done better than they are. This can, however, put you at odds with other people and make you a target for enemies. Although you are fearless, sometimes you may need to temper your opinions to fit in with the more conservative crowd.

Being born between the 31st of March and the 10th of April makes you proud, loyal and sometimes inflexible in your opinions. You have a very strong idea about how life should be lived and you're not prepared to make concessions to others. You are, however, very charming and love to stand out in the crowd. The way you dress, your appearance and your reputation are extremely important to you. You are also very competitive and this aspect of your nature can, like the first group of Aries just mentioned, make you a target for those who become envious of your successful and unique approaches. You may need to employ a little humility to smooth out some of the more difficult relationships in your life.

Being born between the 11th and the 20th of April means you have a broad mind and a full, open heart. This gives you spiritual as well as material ambitions and you will look at life differently to most Aries; indeed, to most people in general. The thrill of travelling and the excitement of exploring the world and alternative cultures mean you'll be plugged into news, current affairs and other topics that give you a deeper understanding of the world. Progressing and expanding your mind, educating yourself and sharing noble ideas with others will make you happy and fulfilled. You certainly have something to teach people and this will be an important component of your destiny.

Aries role model: Heath Ledger

Famous Aussie actor Heath Ledger was born under Aries, just like you. His drive to be the best pushed him to the limits, though. He was an inspiration to fellow actors and, after his death, he received a posthumous Academy Award for his superb work. Heath's enthusiasm for life reflects the true Aries character.

Aries: The light side

Because you exude strength, people are naturally drawn to your power and you inspire them with your courageous leadership.

You are not afraid of challenges or setbacks in life and realise that this approach is what toughens up a human being. This, you believe, is what makes us better people.

Your honesty is often brutal but usually others accept it because they know that you speak from the heart. As well, no one will ever be in doubt as to where they stand with you. You also have great self-confidence and the courage of your convictions. There's rarely, if ever, any deception about the way you interact with those around you. Aries, you are down to earth in all of your dealings.

You are generous and like sharing everything with people and, although you are competitive, there is a part of you that likes to see others be successful as well. You must, however, slow down a little if you want to be a better mentor to your peers.

Aries: The shadow side

Your leadership strengths can turn to aggressiveness if others try to question your authority. You need to be gentler in your assertiveness if you are to win others' hearts, along with their respect. If you need to assert yourself, learn the lesson of doing so without breaking people's spirits. It would be a tragedy if people respected you only because they feared you. Remember, you can earn respect through love.

Aries, you can't always be right all the time, even though mostly you turn out to be correct. You must never let your ego get in the road of smooth, functioning relationships. By tempering your ego, you'll enjoy the best that others have to offer as well.

Sometimes you're excessive and go overboard. Because you try to impress, you can overshoot the mark and fall down. If this happens, you could produce a result opposite to the one you desire.

Because your Aries temperament is so fast, being ruled by the speedy planet Mars, you mustn't become frustrated and angry when those who are slower than you can't keep up with your pace. Furthermore, if others feel as though you're breathing down their necks, lashing out at them with your whip because they're not quite quick enough, you certainly won't bring out the best in them, will you? Obviously they feel nervous with you around. Give people room to breathe and to explore their talents at their own pace rather than coming down hard on them. This will result in a win–win situation.

Aries woman

Aries women are incredibly strong. Although they possess a masculine power, it's wrapped up in a blanket of assertive elegance. Because of this, you have the best of both worlds: grace and power all in one!

As an Aries woman, you're determined to prove that you can achieve ambitions equal to any man or woman and, in fact, will often outdo your rivals. You are focused on your goals and will usually be successful due to your robust Aries personality.

Aries like to be the centre of attention and love it when others concentrate on them fully when they speak or act. Don't lose your focus when dealing with an Aries woman, because she just doesn't have the time to muck around. She's always cramming as much as she can into her busy day. Hers is a full timetable, so you'll need to fit in with her and give her 100 per cent of your attention.

If you're born under Aries, you'll want to be at the top of your game. You won't be satisfied playing second best because this is too frustrating. Biding your time in a stepping-stone position, so to speak, will constrain your spirit. But if you have to wait, you will. Many Aries women who are executives or leaders in their fields started at the bottom of the ladder, working their way up and using their competitiveness to achieve their goals.

Even if you're a stay-at-home mum, you want to be great—not just good—at what you do, and will attempt to do your job better than the next woman. Try to develop more serenity with family members and those who are not quite as capable as you. Learn to set yourself reasonable timelines so you can get everything done without panicking. Sometimes it seems as if everyone else is moving way too slowly, but actually it's you who is moving at breakneck speeds compared with others.

You could become quite stressed if you're not careful, Aries. You live a full existence and cram heaps of work and social activities into your already busy schedule. I suggest you give yourself some quality time to unwind and pamper yourself on a regular basis. It's important to slow the pace; enjoy the journey, not just the goal. Smell the roses on the way. You deserve to give yourself some of the finer things in life rather than postponing your happiness for a rainy day.

Integrity will play a large part in your life. We mentioned earlier the brutal honesty that you employ in dealing with others. It's just part of your nature to be straightforward and you demand that same straightforwardness in return, even if the truth hurts. When you say something, you mean it. You'd prefer to be blunt than risk any sort of misunderstanding, even if you become unpopular. Unfortunately, some Aries women are. This is usually because friends can sometimes become envious.

Your friendships don't always go as smoothly as you'd like them to, especially if you're trying too hard to dominate others. Remember that 'no man or woman is an island unto themselves', and an important part of life is how well you interact with others. The principle of give and take is the best advice I can offer you as an Aries woman.

Compromising sometimes makes you feel as though it's going to kill you. But unless you pursue a path of sharing and allowing for others' shortcomings or weaknesses, you won't gain the full measure of satisfaction possible for a woman like yourself born under Aries.

Aries man

Not all Aries men are as macho as traditional astrology books would like people to believe, but most are. Raw, unbridled power and passion are primary Arian trademarks. You know this firsthand if you're an Aries male or are someone close to them who has experienced their Aries fire.

Aries has the potential to achieve a great deal. With your in-built strength, determination and creativity carefully blended together, it gives you a great fighting chance of realising your dreams. Most Aries do achieve something of note due to these very positive character traits.

Aries who don't fulfil their ambition remain frustrated but they rarely give up, no matter how hard the going gets. You are the proverbial 'battler' and soldier on through thick or thin, rain or hail.

When the going does get tough, this is when your Aries power reaches its pinnacle and shows us what you're really made of.

On the other hand, you're a family man who protects your loved ones and enjoys providing shelter and security. Your loyalty and friendship make you a great partner and a rock-solid support for close friends and family members. People can rely on you to be there for them when difficulties become too much.

You're able to fight for a cause, especially if you see any sort of injustice or an emergency, when you're one of the first to step in and lend a helping hand. People can rely on you because they know your word is honourable.

But you're also demanding, Aries! At times you can be combative and even overbearing in your manner. Let others have their say and don't punish them if they prove you wrong. You have a tendency to believe that, because you have a smattering of knowledge, you must necessarily be correct on all points of difference.

Your youthful vigour also reflects a strong sexual appetite and you need to manage your testosterone levels very carefully. Doing physical exercise is the best suggestion I can offer for you to balance and direct your primal urges in the most beneficial way. There's no doubt that the Aries male has strong carnal appetites that need to be checked from time to time, and physical activity is the best way to unleash your Martian power.

You have incredible drive and stamina and rarely fail to achieve your objectives. While most others fall by the wayside, the Aries man keeps going and going and going. Others are amazed at your ability to persist and continue until your chosen destination is reached.

As an Aries male, you are able to repeatedly prove yourself to others and people easily recognise your worth and power. You like to surround yourself with people who reinforce your self-esteem. There's no doubt that you will take on the role of leader, regardless of what you choose to do in life. You'll be a great example to others, but do try to manage that strong ego of yours.

Aries child

Parents, please note that you can now cancel your gym membership if you have an Aries child: you're not going to need it anymore! Why? Aries is fast-paced, energetic and forever on the go. Can you keep up with them? Not completely, but at least every day will now be a new work-out for you, won't it, because Mars rules their speed, force and relentless drive.

Your Aries child is adventurous, too, but this makes them somewhat accident prone. They want to explore the world and understand everything about it. They're challenging by nature, but if you give them the time, energy and information to satisfy their curiosity, you'll soon find just how clever and intelligent they are.

You'll need closed-circuit TV monitors in a dozen different locations to stay on top of their curious and sometimes wilful activities. Aries kids can be rather wild. Because young Aries children burn the candle at both ends, I also advise you to help them develop good sleeping habits. Life with your Aries child may well be trying, but you'll always be amply rewarded for sharing your love with them.

One simple solution to help overcome these initial problems with your Aries child is to give them a clear-cut regime with a schedule of activities that will capture their attention and imagination. Tire them out with physical exercise and a couple of intense sporting programs; that is, before they wear you out and drive you into the ground!

You must teach them the lesson of sharing power. Because they are such strong little personalities, other kids might resent them if they forcibly try to control playtime. You may need to curb their egos a little to teach them the practicality of relating to others.

Don't argue with your Aries child because there will be no end to it. They will always want to win. Imagine that: a fully grown adult trying to win a battle of wills with a three year old! This happens with many children, but Aries are such seasoned soldiers at it by the time they start walking, you'd better get your bulletproof armour on now.

Romance, love and marriage

There'll never be a dull moment with an Aries in

any sort of relationship, but romance is particularly important to them. Their blazing fires of love are fanned by the winds of sexuality and intimacy.

Mars is bold and straightforward by nature. In your friendships, you keep no secrets about how you feel about another person. You don't see any sense in beating around the bush or playing mind games. This is just not your Aries way. To you, time is of the essence and you want to get down to the nuts and bolts of any friendship or relationship once you feel attracted to another person.

Love and sex are a scintillating and fun game for you and, once the playfulness of a relationship diminishes, sometimes you don't feel at all inspired to continue. For non-Arians reading this, the message is clear. If you venture into love with an Aries native, keep the flames of passion burning brightly, otherwise all is lost.

Many Arians have a very short attention span, which means your partner must keep up the variety of love and make this the heart of the relationship to maintain your interest. You'll enjoy the fun of role-playing because Aries is a young sign, and the idea of growing old is abhorrent to you. Even middle-aged and older Arians enjoy the zest and youthfulness of sexual play.

Being spontaneous, you like spur of the moment outings and events. If the mood catches you, you'll be out the door at the drop of a hat. Hopefully your partner will be able to keep up with your ad hoc antics. There's nothing worse in your mind than someone who acts like a wet blanket and fears getting up and doing something deliciously creative or spontaneous. You must never become involved with someone like this. It will crush your romantic spirit.

You like to be the centre of the universe and will want a lover who builds up your ego, at least initially. Once you do happen to find Mr or Mrs Right, you'll display your affection in return and can be extremely loyal and loving to them.

You defend your honour in love and cannot handle being betrayed. You're such an honest person yourself that you'd rather hear the raw, naked truth, even if it kills you, than have to deal with any form of deception.

But you're not likely to roll over and simply take it if someone crosses you, though. The word 'Aries' is synonymous with the word 'fight'. You will want to have the last word in any confrontation and can make your point quite clearly when that's called for.

Because of the intense energies that Aries generates, you must choose your partner carefully. You need a special person in your life who is sensitive to your needs and will stay committed for the long haul.

Falling in love for you may centre on the game of conquest, and the thrill of the chase will always fascinate you. And if your partner plays hard to get, you love the challenge of winning their heart. Moreover, if someone is competing with you in love, you will work even harder at beating your competitor to win your lover's hand.

Unfortunately, this sporting approach to romance might cause problems if every relationship you chase only ends up adding to a long string of casual associations. At the heart of this is your insatiable desire to be loved and prove that you are a bigger and better lover than everyone else. It's necessary for you to discover what is meaningful in your relationships by finding enough inner security to make them fulfilling and, more importantly, enduring.

Some of your best star sign combinations are with such fire signs as Leo and Sagittarius, or even with air signs like Gemini or Libra. These individuals will nourish your romantic as well as sexual appetites. There is never a hard and fast rule about the people you meet, but through trial and error, astrology has found that these star signs are more than likely most compatible with you.

Finally, you are an excellent home-maker who will protect your family and build a solid, secure foundation for the clan. Protection is one of your in-built instincts towards those you love and care for. Your future should be happy once you connect with your soulmate.

Health, wellbeing and diet

Aries-born individuals are vital and possess abundant physical resources as well as recuperative powers. You are resilient, intense and possess tremendous stamina.

For the most part you're impervious to pain or harsh environmental conditions and can withstand illness and other physical traumas better than most people. Sickness doesn't keep you down for long, even if it does happen to hit you.

Aries have a tendency to overwork or at times do work that is not in keeping with their physical or personality type. Doing this is a no-no because health problems will arise from any mismatched emotional and physical combinations. You mustn't become a workaholic, so listen to your body's signals for they will hint at what you're doing or not doing well. Stop if you are overtired and take adequate rest.

You must never eat on the run, Aries. Set aside enough time to savour each and every morsel of food you eat. And don't skimp on meals. Keep some fruit and nuts with you so that when you do feel overworked or hungry, you can snack on healthy titbits.

You enjoy exotic, spicy and hot foods, which can overstimulate your system. This is not a great idea, so try to be moderate with Indian, Thai and other curry or chilli dishes. You need to temper, not stimulate, the Aries fire.

Green, leafy vegetables and raw foods rich in nutrients such as vitamins and minerals are great boosters for the Arian diet. You need a constant source of great food, which is fuel for your high metabolic rate.

You must never eat when angry or emotionally upset. This is not at all good for anyone's health, Arians and non-Arians alike.

Because coffee, tea, nicotine and alcohol also stimulate your system, it's best to avoid them in case they become bad habits that are deleterious to your health.

Work

Aries individuals are tireless workers with large ambitions. Your need to work is a key component of your life. As an Arian you want to feel as if you are contributing something of value to the world.

Mixing up your routine gives you a greater sense of creativity. You need that variety as part of your professional existence. Being mobile broadens your horizons, for it also gives you a sense of independence and freedom. You need that freedom to feel fulfilled in your work, and hate it if someone can pull your strings as if you're some sort of puppet in the hands of a ventriloquist.

You are highly dextrous, Aries, so working with your hands in any construction, building or engineering pursuit is good for you.

Other professional fields that you might want to consider as a career path include the army or any military or defence force, the police force, security, the sports industry or sales and marketing.

A career in the health sector, a fitness instructor or anything else requiring an entrepreneurial flair is perfect for Aries because you are good in business and also have a highly enterprising spirit.

Key to karma, spirituality and emotional balance

Sagittarius and Jupiter rule your past incarnation. Leo and the Sun rule your future destiny. Therefore, these lucky signs and planets indicate that generosity, open-heartedness and compassion are the keys to your worldly as well as spiritual fulfilment.

'I am' is your key phrase, being born under Aries. This is not the ego 'I am', but a creative presence of being. Relaxing and enjoying the moment will reveal the truth of this key personal phrase for you.

Mondays, Sundays, Tuesdays and Thursdays are lucky for any of your spiritual and self-development pursuits. Spend some time every day slowing your pace to achieve happiness. In turn this will generate better luck for you.

Your lucky days

Your luckiest days are Monday, Tuesday, Thursday and Sunday.

Your lucky numbers

Remember that the forecasts given later in this book will help optimise your chances of winning. Your lucky numbers are:

9, 18, 27, 36, 45, 54

1, 10, 19, 28, 37, 46

3, 12, 21, 30, 48, 57

Your destiny years

Your most important years are 9, 18, 27, 36, 45, 54, 63, 72, and 81.

Star Sign Compatibility

Don't frown because you never know who is falling in love with your smile.

—Sinvyest Tan

Romantic compatibility

How compatible are you with your current partner, lover or friend? Did you know that astrology can reveal a whole new level of understanding between people simply by looking at their star sign and that of their partner? In this chapter I'd like to share some special insights that will help you better appreciate your strengths and challenges using Sun sign compatibility.

The Sun reflects your drive, willpower and personality. The essential qualities of two star signs blend like two pure colours, producing an entirely new colour. Relationships, similarly, produce their own emotional colours when two people interact. The following is a general guide to your romantic prospects with others and how, by knowing the astrological 'colour' of each other, the art of love can help you create a masterpiece.

When reading the following I ask you to remember that no two star signs are ever *totally* incompatible. With effort and compromise, even the most 'difficult' astrological matches can work. Don't close your mind to the full range of life's possibilities! Learning about each other and ourselves is the most important facet of astrology.

Each star sign combination is followed by the

elements of those star signs and the results of their combining. For instance, Aries is a fire sign and Aquarius is an air sign, and this combination produces a lot of 'hot air'. Air feeds fire and fire warms air. In fact, fire requires air. However, not all air and fire combinations work. I have included information about the different birth periods within each star sign and this will throw even more light on your prospects for a fulfilling love life with any star sign you choose.

Good luck in your search for love, and may the stars shine upon you in 2011!

Compatibility quick-reference guide

Each of the twelve star signs has a greater or lesser affinity with one another. The quick-reference guide will show you who's hot and who's not so hot as far as your relationships are concerned.

ARIES + ARIES

Fire + Fire = Explosion

Have you ever seen two rams locking horns? For a while, their frolicking and play looks like a lot of fun, until they get too competitive and start butting heads together. As you're aware, the ram is the Aries totem. This simply means that, in this relationship, the two of you are likely to lock horns, going head to head on many occasions because you both feel you are completely correct on most matters.

Quick-reference guide: Horoscope compatibility between signs (percentage)

	Aries	Taurus	Gemini	Cancer	Leo	Virgo	Libra	Scorpio	Sagittarius	Capricorn	Aquarius	Pisces
Aries	60	65	65	65	90	45	70	80	90	50	55	65
Taurus	60	70	70	80	70	90	75	85	50	95	80	85
Gemini	70	70	75	60	80	75	90	60	75	50	90	50
Cancer	65	80	60	75	70	75	60	95	55	45	70	90
Leo	90	70	80	70	85	75	65	75	95	45	70	75
Virgo	45	90	75	75	75	70	80	85	70	95	50	70
Libra	70	75	90	60	65	80	80	85	80	85	95	50
Scorpio	80	85	60	95	75	85	85	90	80	65	60	95
Sagittarius	90	50	75	55	95	70	80	85	85	55	60	75
Capricorn	50	95	50	45	45	95	85	65	55	85	70	85
Aquarius	55	80	90	70	70	50	95	60	60	70	80	55
Pisces	65	85	50	90	75	70	50	95	75	85	55	80

Aries is a very powerful sign of the zodiac, and therefore your willpower will be equally as strong as your partner's. By willpower I am of course referring to the Aries ego, which is very unyielding. You and your Aries partner can expect many clashes of ego unless one of you is prepared to concede that you are not always 100 per cent right all the time.

This relationship does have the hallmarks of a positive and successful alliance, notwithstanding the fact that you are both dynamic individuals. Your ruling planet Mars promises many exciting opportunities to develop your love. Fortunately much of your time together will be based on gracious competition rather than a desire to hurt each other. This sporting attitude is probably one of the stronger elements binding you together.

Because Aries is childlike and enthusiastic, a happy social life with many fun times together can be expected. The two of you form a dynamic duo and will take the lead at social events. In combination you are also very extroverted and creative, so that your vibrant liveliness stimulates your family and friends.

You are passionate in the way you approach love and friendship and, as lovers, you will understand and inspire each other with your constant desire for love and affection. As long as you are both prepared to share being the centre of attention, your love will grow over time. And also don't forget that Aries is a very independent sign, so don't try to smother each other by being possessive. This won't work. The two of you need ample time to explore your own individual interests.

Your strong passion and sexual yearnings make the Aries–Aries love match a very physical one. You'll be extremely attracted to each other and sex will be a key component of keeping the flame of love alive. Because the element of fire brings out your deeper, lustful instincts, you will enjoy many exciting and sensual times together. However, you also have a tendency to be excessive in this area. You will always continue to explore your love and passion, so although there are some pitfalls in this relationship, the overall outcome is quite fulfilling.

Partying, enjoying friends and outdoor activities will be the hallmarks of a relationship with another Aries born between the 31st of March and the 10th of April. You will definitely enjoy life together, and I don't see any sort of boredom setting in because you are both constantly on the go. You have a strong sexual attraction for each other, and the creative energy you contribute to this relationship will also bring you both considerable satisfaction.

Try not to let your hot-headed temper get the better of you, especially if you are attracted to another Aries born between the 21st and the 30th of March. This is a powerful love match that might prove to be awkward for you. Remain cool under pressure, even when your partner provokes you.

All Aries innately understand their counterparts born under the same star sign. However, a combination with those born between the 11th and the 20th of April is fortunate for marriage and romance generally. This is due to the strong Jupiter–Sagittarius influence during this period. The karmic forecast for the two of you with this combination is very good, and your financial circumstances should also improve due to this match.

ARIES + TAURUS

Fire + Earth = Lava

The ram and the bull are an extreme combination of energies, so this love match may or may not work. Sometimes it's great, yet at other times it's challenging, to say the least.

If you choose a partner who is born under Taurus you can expect a deeply loyal and loving partner who is also passionate in the right circumstances. I have found there is a natural attraction between both of your star signs due to the Mars–Venus influence on both of you.

Taurus is a plodding and methodical star sign compared to Aries. Therefore your impatience could create problems for this relationship if you don't give Taurus the latitude to follow their own course, at their own pace.

Taurus is a wilful sign and needs things to be done on its own terms. Because you also like to control situations, there will be points in time where each of you needs to concede to allow the other to be the leader, in turns. This will work as a happy compromise for the Aries and Taurus combination.

You respect the Taurus willpower and their commitment towards achieving their ambitions. You can work well together to create a happy and secure lifestyle for yourselves and your family if you make the decision to connect with each other over the long term.

Taurus is an excellent moneymaker and likes what money can buy. For both of you, finance and sharing your material resources will be a strong point in your favour, but it's probably better to let your Taurus partner have a majority control in money issues.

Taurus is sensible, stable and very well grounded in practical matters. You will feel comfortable and secure entrusting many affairs of your life to them, including your finances.

You are not accustomed to people challenging you too much, but you'll be surprised when the bull of the zodiac, Taurus, takes up your challenge. Taurus doesn't immediately show the full power of their anger. Rest assured that, if provoked, you will soon realise you have met your match. The bull can be quite a fierce animal.

Your sexual interaction with Taurus will be sensual and very passionate. This is because they are ruled by Venus, the planet of love. You won't have many complaints about their sensual responses, other than the fact that they are a little slow off the mark in demonstrating their feelings compared with you. Exercise some initial patience and your desires will then be fully satisfied by your Taurus mate.

Taurean lovers can be possessive and also demanding. Make a mental note of that before you go off flirting at the next party you're both invited to. Don't take Taurus's trust for granted.

Your Taurus partner is extremely well suited to you and your friendship will grow over time if they were born between the 21st and the 29th of April. Venus creates a great deal of passion between you, so this astrological combination is even quite well suited for marriage.

Your communication is stimulated by a Taurus lover born between the 30th of April and the 10th of May. This is because of the influence of Mercury in combination with Venus. You greatly enjoy each other's company and will spend considerable time sharing ideas and planning for the future.

There's a strong spiritual and karmic connection if you team up with someone born between the 11th and the 21st of May. So if you're looking for your star mate, this could be them.

ARIES + GEMINI

Fire + Air = Hot Air

The elements of fire and air make an excellent combination, astrologically speaking, so a love affair between Aries and Gemini is likely to work extremely well.

Your partner, your Gemini, lives primarily in the realm of the mind and requires a great deal of intellectual stimulation. This the fire sign of

Aries is able to provide. Yours is a reciprocal arrangement, and you'll never tire of the brilliant communication skills of your Gemini mate.

At times the Aries temperament is a little brash and requires refinement when dealing with Gemini. Gemini is acutely sensitive to the opinions of Aries, which are sometimes rather blunt. Turn it down and try to be a little less brutal in your opinions when dealing with them.

Gemini will stimulate your curious and passionate temperament as well as fulfilling your sexual needs. The combination of air and fire elements is an excellent one for the bedroom. The Gemini quality of air will fan the flames of your passion and make for wonderful social and sexual times together.

Gemini is one of the few star signs that have an extraordinarily great sense of humour, even as they age. You can expect the odd prank or practical joke with them, which is just the way they keep themselves young and also try to stimulate others.

Your love life with Gemini will not be immune to problems. But with regular communication and an open sensitivity to their needs, you'll be able to overcome any problems that do arise and grow in love together. Try to pay more attention to the subtleties of any situation and remember that Gemini, when nervous, tends to chatter more than you would prefer. Don't be dismissive of them, however, because this will deeply hurt their feelings.

Aries and Gemini make excellent mates, not just great lovers. In this way, such a combination is a plus for any sort of romantic involvement. Not only will you be lovers but you will be great buddies. Your social lives will constantly be busy. And, sexually speaking, a Gemini will inspire you, both mentally and physically.

There is an argumentative streak with those Geminis born between the 22nd of May and the 1st of June. Regrettably your compatibility quotient is not all that strong with this group.

With a Gemini partner born anywhere between the 2nd and the 12th of June, you are compatible romantically and socially. This is a robust relationship and will provide you both with sexual satisfaction and excellent communication. Sexuality will be an important component of your partnership with them.

Geminis born between the 13th and the 21st of June are not particularly well suited to you sexually, but could become great supporters of you at the level of friendship. Enjoy yourselves socially before committing yourself on any other level. Dedicate quality time to getting to know each other. Your first impressions may not be correct and it would be a shame for you to miss out on a deeper and more enjoyable relationship together.

ARIES + CANCER

Fire + Water = Steam

Cancer is one of the softer and more accommodating signs of the zodiac. Their ruler the Moon is particularly friendly to Mars, which happens to govern the sign of Aries.

Cancer's sensitive energies counteract your fiery and sometimes blunt personality. The elements of fire and water, respectively belonging to Aries and Cancer, are very different but nonetheless they can work positively for you. This is particularly the case on the domestic front, because this is where Cancer feels most at home.

Always compassionate and forgiving, these tender and sensitive souls will provide you with considerable affection and love. However, you must never treat them harshly or you can deeply and permanently wound them. And the problem is, you may never know this has happened, because they also tend to be rather secretive and don't always reveal their hand.

Cancer is one of the most caring and nourishing of the star signs and, if you're looking for a happy family life, Cancer will satisfy you immensely in this respect.

Those born under Cancer are very adaptable individuals and can change with the times, adjusting to your needs. Don't mistake this for any sort of weakness, however. You will be surprised by their resilience and strength of purpose.

Your passion will be an excellent motivation to Cancer, but try not to be too pushy with them. As long as you adapt yourself to their sensitive and intuitive approach to life, you will be able to make considerable headway in your relationship together.

The Aries and Cancer match is an excellent one for family life and highlights the archetypal symbols of masculinity and femininity coming together. These two polarities work well and can fulfil you both over the long term.

Sexually you will need to try harder to understand your Cancer partner's needs. Be soft, gentle and affectionate with them, and they will show you a love you probably haven't experienced before. By remaining aware of their emotional sensitivities, the relationship will become more satisfying for both of you.

If you team up with a Cancer born between the 22nd of June and the 2nd of July, curb your stubborn approach. These are very thin-skinned people who need extra tender loving care and attention. However, expect loads of affection from them if you give them time and energy.

Cancerians born between the 3rd and the 13th of July are intense individuals and, in a relationship with them, you'll meet your match. This is a powerful love relationship. Their passionate energy will stimulate you sexually and mentally.

A relationship with a Cancer born between the 14th and the 23rd of July may not satisfy you sexually and their idealism seems way too impractical for your taste. A spiritual association is more likely to be the result if you are that way inclined.

ARIES + LEO

Fire + Fire = Explosion

The explosive power of an Aries and Leo combination is undeniable and needs considerable taming before the relationship can find its feet. Leo has a greater capacity to manage this power than you do and is also able to help you realise your full potential. This really is one of the best love matches in the zodiac. Your attraction to each other is obvious. Your relationship with Leo will be very satisfying on almost every level.

The Aries–Leo relationship is built on a solid foundation of friendship. Because you're both ruled by the same fiery element, you share an easygoing attitude with each other and have an instinctive understanding of each other's needs. This is a great boost.

Leo is a proud star sign and they need to have considerable leeway when 'strutting their stuff'. As long as you don't get in their road and cramp their style, they'll be fine. But, Aries, you do have a large ego as well, so you could find it hard playing second fiddle to your Leo counterpart.

The Sun and Mars rule your star signs respectively and are considered excellent friends in the zodiac scheme of things. They are both male planets, which indicates your relationship will be full of power and vitality. You like the outdoors and a great deal of physical activity, which will serve the relationship well.

However, you must remember that Leo is very inflexible on certain matters. Trying to change their minds will not be that easy. You must also be aware you're not always going to be the boss in the house. Sharing power is a vital issue between Leos and Aries. As long as you can learn the art of give and take, the relationship will work well in the domestic situation.

Your sexual experience with Leo is satisfying, if not electrifying. This really is an almost perfect match between the sheets. You'll be able to fulfil each other's desires, both physically and emotionally. There's an instinctive understanding of what you each need and you'll make the effort to ensure your partner's satisfied.

Your relationship with a Leo born between the 24th of July and the 3rd of August highlights the need for the two of you to work hard at sharing power in your domestic circumstance. You are both very strong-willed and may try to outdo each other. Although this is not an easy combination, it can still bring you a great deal of satisfaction.

Another great match is with Leos born between the 4th and the 13th of August. If you believe in reincarnation, this combination shows that there was unfinished business between you in your previous lives. This time around you should be quite lucky together.

Pretty much all Leos will be suitable in a relationship with you, but those born between the 14th and the 23rd of August are an excellent choice in love. You'll see a great deal of yourselves in each other. This is a stimulating combination sexually. It can be light-hearted, thrilling and fun.

ARIES + VIRGO

Fire + Earth = Lava

It's never easy for me to say that two star signs are not well suited, but in this case, I have to admit there are some difficulties. However, they're not totally insurmountable. Initially you don't particularly feel that comfortable with each other, but with some compromise and work, you may be able to make the Aries–Virgo match somewhat satisfying.

Your Virgo partner is less outgoing and prefers to sit back behind the scenes rather than stealing the show. In that sense, Virgos will allow you full rein to be the centre of attention. There'll be no competition with them; in fact, they are happy to support and help you become as popular as you can be.

Virgos like to aim for perfection and this is one quality in them that you admire. But they may also come across as a little too obsessive-compulsive in their attention to detail, which is where you may run headlong into difficulties. Your approach to your daily routine may be very different to theirs, so yet again, patience will be the order of the day.

The fire signs like Aries are quite spontaneous and creative, and here is another difference between you and your Virgo partner. Virgos like to take as long as possible to draw their conclusions. You see this as dithering and will be annoyed if they can't come to the point much more quickly. However, don't be so headstrong with them. Perhaps you can teach them the art of relying more on intuition than on sheer brainpower.

You're an up-front sort of individual, in particular when it comes to sexual matters. You'll need to understand that Virgos are more withdrawn and prefer to take the time to get to know others before sharing their deeper emotions and physical passions. But once a Virgo gives themselves to you, you'll be surprised at their versatility and ingenuity in lovemaking.

Virgos are as generous as you are. Therefore the two of you can share much in common and enjoy the benefits that come through selflessly loving another. Virgos will offer their support to you in any of your life's endeavours and will be genuinely happy for your success.

Virgos born between the 24th of August and the 2nd of September are quite well suited to you, so it's worthwhile considering them as friends and lovers. Don't be too harsh a judge of these Virgos, however, because they may simply be a little more complicated than other people to work out.

You could run into some serious problems with Virgos born between the 3rd and the 12th of September. Spend some additional time getting to know these individuals before committing yourself to them. This is not a great combination.

If you have an attraction to Virgos born between the 13th and the 23rd of September, your relationship should be quite good. In the cluster of Virgos, these are definitely the ones best suited to you. You will support each other well, particularly in business matters.

ARIES + LIBRA

Fire + Air = Hot Air

Aries and Libra lovers are often attracted to each other due to the strong connection between Mars and Venus, which are the planets that rule these star signs.

Mars rules passion and Venus sensuality, so is it any wonder that the two of you experience such warmth and vitality when in each other's company? Also, because Libra represents your marital zone of the horoscope, we can't rule out the question of marriage or a long-term relationship between the two of you.

Libra is much more strong-willed than you can at first imagine. It's not a well-known fact, but this cultured and creative star sign can be quite combative and revolutionary. If they are born towards the cast of Scorpio, you will find out they are particularly intense and demanding.

Both of you are very busy and changeable in nature. Tying down either of you will not be easy. Set your appointments and your schedules together when you can, so there will be no conflict or possibility that an argument will arise later on because you're not seeing each other. You need to make decisions about this relationship mutually.

Aries is sometimes a little hard to get to know. Libra is quite a sociable star sign and needs lots of open space to explore relationships. If either of you becomes possessive or jealous of the other's time and friends, this relationship will fall apart. Allow each other some independence to grow individually.

Libra is as passionate as Aries, but in a more refined manner. The two of you enjoy making love because your passions are in sync with each other. Libra, the cardinal air sign of the zodiac, feeds not only the fires of your love but also your anger in equal proportions. You are both opinionated but can use your lovemaking to temper this tendency to clash.

Attraction comes easily for you with Librans born between the 24th of September and the 3rd of October. Your association will quickly develop into a powerful romance, all things being equal. Your ruling planets work well together and provide considerable compatibility.

Your relationship with Librans born between the 4th and the 13th of October will be quite special. This will be a strong and lasting relationship, but it also comes with a great deal of responsibility. It's quite likely you'll spend a long time together. Integrity is one of the key words for this match.

Librans born between the 14th and the 23rd of October are not as practical or grounded as you would like them to be. Due to the rulership of their birth date by both Venus and Mercury, they tend to be scattered in their approach and need some gentle direction.

ARIES + SCORPIO

Fire + Water = Steam

The Aries and Scorpio love relationship is one of the more powerful of the zodiac matches. Although the elements ruling the two of you are very different, fire and water, you are still very attracted to each other and will experience many common interests and states of mind.

Scorpio has the magnetic power to draw you to them, and they might not necessarily do this through their words. Their gestures and in particular their hypnotic eyes are enough to win your heart. You are awestruck by Scorpio. It's okay to admit that, but at the same time you'll consciously need to keep some distance to understand the depths of their power. You must never underestimate a Scorpio's ability to retaliate if you cross them.

Common characteristics that both of you share include drive, passion and high aspirations. This is because Mars is a common ruling planet for both of your star signs. Scorpio, however, also has the added influence of deep, secretive and transformative Pluto and is less open about revealing their feelings. Don't push them to share their dark secrets with you until they are ready, or you might just scare them away. They are deep, brooding and sometimes unforgiving if pushed to the limit.

Scorpios can be manipulative in relationships. They know what they want and they demand it on their own terms, which means you may meet your match in the Scorpio personality. Scorpio doesn't live life or love by normal standards, and you need to get used to this. However, if you're prepared to play by their rules, you will experience new dimensions in love.

Your sincere outlook is attractive to Scorpio, even if he or she doesn't openly admit it. And remember, Scorpios have a suspicious nature and will often test your devotion to them. Don't prove them correct because you might not get a second chance with them.

Your head-to-head confrontations can be counteracted by tender, loving sessions. Make time for each other so that passionate Mars and Pluto can work together to deepen the love and sensuality you share. Scorpio will inspire you sexually because they are masters in the art of love.

Scorpios are generally secretive; however, the cusp Scorpio who is born between the 24th of October and the 4th of November is more conversational than your typical Scorpio. These characters have an opinion on anything and everything and there may be quite a few disagreements between you.

Scorpios born between the 5th and the 14th of November are romantic and you'll be fascinated by them. However, you need adventure and freedom and that may not be provided by them. They are psychological in nature and need loads of mental stimulation.

Scorpios born between the 15th and the 22nd of November have a Piscean quality to them and will trigger your spiritual nature. They are an excellent match if you are interested in self-development.

ARIES + SAGITTARIUS

Fire + Fire = Explosion

As with the Aries–Leo combination, the fire sign of Sagittarius joined with Aries creates a great match that brings vitality, a spirit of adventure and also the tendency for a long-term relationship for the two of you.

This fiery combination is fuelled by natural attraction but also comes with variety and what some might call 'a handful of spice' thrown in for good measure. The two of you may be so busily engaged in exploring the world that settling down may not be exactly high on either of your agendas. You'll both need to burn up some of your surplus hot fuel before becoming homebodies.

Spontaneity is at the core of this relationship, and brings great satisfaction to the two of you in your connection. You both have the knack of understanding—in the moment—what the other wants to do. Therefore, going out, staying home or generally just lazing about will all be activities in which you are simultaneously in sync with each other.

But in Sagittarius there is a philosophy of life that says one should never regret not having tried something. There's a child-like quality to both of your personalities, which is why your life experiences are so full of thrills and sometimes spills. If you happen to look back on the road of life you've chosen together, you will do so with a great deal of satisfaction because you have at least tried something a little different and didn't live life the way most people do. Boredom will never set in with an Aries and Sagittarius partnership.

Sex is very important for the fire signs and you'll each be satisfied that the other has similar needs to yourself. Your appetite is strong, as is your desire to please your partner. Exploring love-making with your Sagittarian mate will augment your compatibility.

Your choice of love with a Sagittarian born between the 23rd of November and the 1st of December is a very good one. The two of you will realise you are probably soulmates who have been waiting, finally, to reconnect. Sagittarians born in this period also provide you with great physical satisfaction.

Sagittarian lovers born between the 2nd and the 11th of December offer you an extremely powerful connection with them as well. They will reflect precisely what you most desire in a life partner. The reason for this is that they possess quite a bit of the same fiery Mars energy that you do.

Sagittarians born between the 12th and the 22nd of December are resolute and even stubborn. You will find them unyielding in their opinions and this will create obstacles if you also possess that stubbornness, too. Flexibility will be the key to making this relationship work.

ARIES + CAPRICORN

Fire + Earth = Lava

Being with a Capricorn is probably difficult for a typical Aries-born individual because of the seriousness of Saturn, their ruler. Capricorn is traditional and sometimes less than vivacious in the eyes of Aries. But because you are quite impulsive and impatient at times, you run the risk of overlooking some of the sterling qualities of your potential Capricorn partner.

Don't let their quiet and sometimes insular aura detract you from some of the other, more stabilising qualities that you most definitely need in your life. Saturn is one of the few star signs that can pin you to the ground, anchor you and keep you focused on what's important in life. This will be even more the case if you are under 30 years of age and are reading this.

With Capricorn, your life will be practical and not always as carefree as you'd like it to be. But the stability they bring to the relationship can offer you the opportunity to explore areas of your life that may not be possible alone or with another star sign. And, of course, you will be a challenge to your Capricorn friend because of your spirit of adventure and impulsiveness, which can really push Capricorn off balance.

Capricorns are very controlling in most areas of their lives, including their relationships, which will be something you'll find hard to accept. You're the boss—or so you thought—until Capricorn came into your world. And arguing with them will be difficult, too, because they don't throw around the same fire and exhibitionism you do. Even when they fight, they do it in a controlled fashion. That can be very frustrating to Aries.

You are very dissimilar sexually and in the way you express yourselves emotionally. This means you will not be particularly suited to physical intimacy. While you enjoy each other's company and have a curiosity about each other, you might need to understand that Aries and Capricorn are just so very different.

Capricorns born between the 23rd of December and the 1st of January are quiet and inward people who don't reflect your personality's needs. They are not particularly exciting and so these Capricorn-born characters may not be your cup of tea.

Capricorns born between the 2nd and the 10th of January are much more sexually and psychologically suited to you because of the Saturn–Venus influence. You'll feel a strong attraction between you and they are far better able to adapt themselves to your fiery nature.

You can experience good communication and mental curiosity with any Capricorn born between the 11th and the 20th of January. Although still not your ideal match, you are somewhat more compatible sexually than the typical Aries–Capricorn match.

ARIES + AQUARIUS

Fire + Air = Hot Air

Aquarians are exciting, progressive individuals who stimulate your desire for change and radical experiences in life, so it's quite likely you'll be attracted to at least one of them at some stage in your life. But the chances are that you, Aries, will also misunderstand them, primarily because you are very different types of people.

Your respective ruling planets, Mars and Uranus, produce an explosive reaction. Although I mentioned that fire and air produces hot air, it's truer to say that this combination of planets is extremely unstable. Thus the prognosis is that anything can happen in your lives together—both good and not so good.

There are times when the two of you can indeed find a common meeting place emotionally, but these occurrences may be few and far between. Autonomy is vitally important for both of you and, although your astrological elements are different, there are a few things you have in common. You both enjoy being part of a social group and you feel as if Aquarius encourages you to express yourself and live your life independently.

Aquarians are very different in the way they live their lives and present their ideas to you. They enjoy life in the fast lane and, with Mars also being fast and volatile, you will find their company very exciting.

You are both very strong-willed individuals and possess large egos. Aquarius uses this to help the world as a whole and make it a better place for all, or so seems to be their aspiration in life. They want to make a difference in the world. They desire someone to help them fulfil this dream. Is that you?

The attraction between Aries and Aquarius is strange, but also sexually alluring. Aquarians aren't afraid to explore what is hidden, those things that are considered taboo in life, and this will turn you on. You're hot and passionate enough to stimulate each other. Just remember that Aquarians have very strong mental needs, too, which extend to their lovemaking rituals.

You are challenged by Aquarians born between the 21st and the 31st of January. You'll discover that they are as determined as you. However, they are not as mentally supple as you and therefore your opinions will often be at odds with each other.

You and Aquarians born between the 1st and the 9th of February can become great mates. You are able to open your heart to them and vice versa. This is a great combination and also satisfies you both socially.

If you team up with an Aquarian born between the 10th and the 19th of February you'll enjoy their great sense of humour and fun. The two of you will also enjoy your sexual experiences together. Venus and Libra strongly rule them, so this is an additional factor working to your advantage.

ARIES + PISCES

Fire + Water = Steam

You can't quite get your head around the Pisces character, even though you may be very attracted to them. There is something about Pisces you can't quite understand, but it's precisely this unqualifiable factor that draws you nearer and nearer to them.

In their company you feel relaxed, soft and sensitive, which is very unlike your true Aries personality. The loving Pisces is a watery, sensitive, dreamy person who tempers your fiery nature. Your sexual connection with Pisces is extremely potent.

But never overlook the fact that Pisces is also very emotional, as shown by the water element ruling them. Unless you are able to offer them the emotional component of love, they will not be totally satisfied with living on only material and physical levels.

It's not likely to be a relationship that can meet either of your expectations in the long run. But strangely you will be attracted to each other and will want to at least find out how you each tick and how the relationship between you may work as well.

Aries and Pisces are karmically destined to meet in an unusual manner and will most likely find themselves either in some hidden affair or a culturally dominating relationship. You will both need to assess how practical the relationship is before you commit yourself to each other too deeply. There can be outside influences opposing your relationship, including friends, family members or just the cultural circumstances in which you live.

Aries individuals are very interested in achieving their material goals, whereas Pisces live life for spiritual and idealistic reasons. Your life philosophies may be at odds because Pisces is rarely interested in material gains but rather in selfless surrender. Take this into account as your relationship develops. Pisces will open your heart and give you glimpses of whole new alternative ways of living.

Pisces is the sign of the zodiac that knows best how to love unconditionally. Sexually they are generous and also very inventive. But a word of warning: never take Pisces for granted or crush their spirit because hurting them will ruin your relationship permanently.

Pisceans born between the 20th and the 28th or 29th of February are rarely compatible with you. The match between you could even result in some health problems because your energies on a spiritual level are not in tune.

With Pisces born between the 1st and the 11th of March your energies are quite compatible and you will feel happy to share your life, wealth and future with them. If you're looking for a cosy and homely life, you may be attracted to these Pisceans.

With Pisces born between the 12th and the 20th of March, expect passion, affection and tenderness as part of the deal in love. The raging flames of passion and sexual desire are strong for the two of you, so this is also an excellent match for the long term.

ARIES

2011:
The Year Ahead

The steeper the mountain, the harder the climb, the better the view from the finishing line.

—Anonymous

Romance and friendship

In spite of some limitations you might feel in your personal life, you'll be confident that 2011 will give you new choices and pathways in your love life and social activities.

Saturn continues to demand greater responsibility in your marriage and other significant relationships. The first three months of 2011 will be particularly intense, with this planet causing you to question your motives in all manner of interactions.

Even if you try to use your charm and persuasion, you may not be successful until after the 7th of January. At this time you'll be luckier in conveying your true feelings to another. And, conversely, they too will be more likely to share their secrets with you.

In February, Venus creates a wonderful atmosphere of love and opportunity in your life. This makes you attractive, loving and popular. This seductive vibration continues throughout February and March. Your ruling planet Mars and the Sun and Neptune conjointly occupy your friendship zone throughout this period as well, indicating that your social activities will be numerous. However, you may also be burning the candle at both ends, so try to pace yourself a little, especially in the earlier part of the year.

Your social life reaches a high in March when Venus comes to your zone of friendship. Love affairs are also indicated; however, should you be already attached to someone, you need to be careful not to send out mixed signals. Even if you think flirting is just a bit of light, casual fun, someone else may take your advances more seriously than you intended them to be. Jupiter initiates a new twelve-month cycle in which you can expand your personal horizons and make a wonderful impact everywhere you go.

Fortunately the combined influence of the Sun and Jupiter is excellent in providing you with lucky opportunities throughout April, and new friendships will arise due to your generous disposition. You're prepared to open your heart, render assistance to others and, although you may not be on the lookout for a relationship, it's quite likely that life will bring you someone interesting with whom to share your feelings and your ideas.

From the end of April through to May, the influence of Venus with Uranus brings you some sudden and unexpected romantic opportunities. You may be caught off-guard and, even if you are excited by the prospect of a new relationship, I suggest you tread warily. What may at first appear to be a completely wonderful match made in heaven could turn out to be short-lived after all.

You are full of dynamism and energy throughout May when your ruling planet Mars, the planet of vitality, physical desire and activity, comes in touch with lucky Jupiter. This is a period of the year when your sense of timing will be impeccable and you should use this to good advantage. You might just happen to be in the right place at the right time if you're looking for love. You're also attractive and easily appeal to the opposite sex, with Venus and the Sun giving you a boost of sensual energy, too.

Luck continues to be a key element in your life. Venus is also lending its assistance to Jupiter, thereby bringing you more than your fair share of windows of opportunity when it comes to love and romance. The main thing at this time—and I don't want to keep harping on Saturn's difficult influence on you—is to use discrimination. You will need to weed out those who are worthy of your love from those who are simply wasting your time.

Passion is usually the result of Venus and Mars in conjunction, which is precisely what you can expect in late May. A solar eclipse early in June shows you may be ready and raring to go in a new relationship, or perhaps revved up to give your current relationship a second chance.

You will see some new developments in your marital life as a result of Saturn moving in a direct motion after the 13th. A lunar eclipse on the 16th compounds these celestial events, making June a very important and busy period for you as far as relationships, family issues and social activities are concerned.

Your attention may be focused more on family matters than your own personal needs and desires at this time as well. Another solar eclipse in July ushers in a month of very important developments in your domestic sphere. Dealing with your mother, siblings and other facets of your personal life on the home front will occupy a large part of your time.

The Sun and Venus prompt you towards creative activities after the 23rd of July. You'll be feeling expansive, fun-loving and desirous of expressing yourself in new and quirky ways. This is the perfect time to combine your creative impulses with love and friendship. Taking up an art class, dancing, or maybe even just going to the cinema; taking time out from your busy schedule and sharing some intimate moments with friends will be great ways to plug you back into the fun side of yourself.

Your inner child will be calling out just now, but your 'outer child'—that is, your children if you're married and parenting—will also demand some extra time throughout August.

Mars may be a problem for you because it can create conflicts on the home front throughout this month. Venus transiting your zone of selfless service also shows that you may have to put your own needs second on your list of priorities because someone else requires your help at this time. Health matters may be a cause for concern, both for yourself and for someone you love. Part of your selfless duty may now be to care for that person as you put aside your own personal interests for a little while.

However, things can get back on track for you in September, with Venus moving into your most important zone of relationships, and with Mars also entering into your sector of love affairs. The Sun also joins the party on the 23rd of September, highlighting September as being an important month to stir up your sexual, emotional and social energies. This will continue quite strongly into October, with Venus and the Sun entering your sexual zone at this time.

Deeper secrets or issues that have been lingering for a while need to be dissolved so that your love life can be transformed into what it should be. One point, too, that should be mentioned, is the combined influence of the Sun and Saturn around the 14th of October. You'll need to pay special attention to where your relationship is headed. This mix of planetary energies usually hints at the fact that you may need to discipline yourself more, and any form of laziness has to be removed from the picture if you're to feel comfortable in love.

This Sun–Saturn influence is particularly telling on relationships or marital arrangements that have gone past their use-by date. You may be feeling that your love is not reciprocated—that you're giving much more than you're receiving—and may simply want a quick exit strategy.

A lighter tone is evident in your affairs after November when Venus enters your lucky ninth house. This imparts to you a sense of adventure, freedom and release. After some of the more complex planetary patterns of the previous months, this will certainly be a relief for you and gives you the opportunity to travel, expand your horizons and do something a little out of the ordinary.

Throughout the remainder of the year, Venus will usher in a new sense of self for you, an energy that may cause you to overhaul your ego and your attitudes to yourself completely. This, of course, will impact on the way others see you, which is precisely what you will want. This could even be called 'a life makeover'.

The connection of Venus to Pluto in December is revolutionary. This is like the proverbial caterpillar emerging from its cocoon and breaking free as a butterfly. At this time of your life, you will be like that butterfly, wanting to spread your wings to fly. If for some reason, in your social or personal life, or even in your marriage, you've felt as if you've been limited, suppressed or unfulfilled, then the jewel in the crown for Arians in 2011, especially in this last part of the year, will be your ability to create a new life and destiny for yourself.

Work and money

It's clear that work will be paramount to Arians throughout 2011. With the Sun, your ruling planet Mars and Pluto occupying your zone of professionalism in the first month of the year, you'll be off to a flying start. A solar eclipse in your zone of work and ambition tells you that you are keenly interested in making some vital changes and will not be satisfied with a mediocre or less-than-stellar success in this year coming.

You can gain through renewed and progressive work practices in February when Mercury and the Sun conjoin Mars in your eleventh zone of profits, social activity and fulfilment. To get ahead of your competitors, you need to be prepared to break new ground and to attempt things you might not have done in the past.

March will be an extremely busy period. With Jupiter moving into your Sun sign, you can expect some good old-fashioned luck to kick in and push your self-efforts forward, and quickly at that. You have energy, optimism and what it takes to start realising the fruits of your hard efforts.

Pay attention to the finer details of contracts and other work issues throughout March. Even if you dislike having to lay low for a while (withstanding the surge of energy that you feel; the impulse that is part of your Arian nature), hold back until you get a clearer picture of what you want. Playing it a little low-key will pay off.

Throughout April, you have immense initiative, shown by your ruling planet Mars arriving back at your Sun sign. You need to focus your energies very clearly and not take on too many things. Stagger your workload, delegate some of the tasks and don't be in such a rush to achieve the end goal. This will also afford you greater peace of mind.

In May and June, you'll be restless and desire some sort of change, particularly in your professional arena. Others may be inhibiting you, particularly with Saturn doing its thing in your zone of public relations and business partnerships. But the lunar eclipse on the 16th of this month gives you a broader vision and makes you feel much more confident that, although others may be cramping your style, the best is yet to come.

You need to take care of your fixed assets and investments throughout June, July and again in August. Mars, your ruler, activates the fourth zone of family and real estate. If you're the sort of person who is a little reluctant to take a punt or gamble on the stock market or other risky investments, June and July should be a time for you to consider how you can best secure your future through solid, earthy projects and investments.

If you're not that way inclined and you are more of a risk-taking Aries-born individual, Mercury's entrance into the fifth zone of speculation around the 7th of August could cause you to take a little more risk than you normally would. Be careful, however, because at this time of the year the Sun transits your zone of debts, which could take you by surprise.

In September, with Mercury entering your sixth zone of work environments, debts and enemies, you need to take a full account of your spending and earning capacity. Balance the account books at this time and, if necessary, learn how to do it properly or pay someone to do it for you, even if they seem a little costly at the time. You'll be surprised when you learn that there are savings that can be made through a proper analysis of your expenditure, which may result in distinct tax benefits as well.

In the last few days of September and into October, the Sun conjoins Mercury in your zone of partnerships. You are clever, have the support of others and may even decide to strike up some sort of new partnership at this stage. You'll be more cautious than normal, however, because Mercury will also be under the influence of Saturn and this means a slower, more steady view of things.

Don't be scared to scrutinise others. Look into their pasts and, by all means, verify the story being given to you. Not everything that is presented will be exactly as it seems, and this could come to light after the 24th of October when the Sun transits your eighth house of joint finances and other people's money. Legal matters throughout November are highlighted by Mercury's entrance into your ninth zone, and you need to word your proposals carefully if you seek bigger and brighter successes.

With Mars in your zone of hard work, health and debt, you could be pushing things a little too hard, which could start to be reflected in a weakened vitality and confused thinking. On the 24th of November, when Mercury goes retrograde, you're advised to hold back from signing any documents, for a couple of good reasons. Firstly, as I just mentioned, your health may not be up to scratch and secondly, certain facts may not yet have been presented to you.

When Mercury goes direct on the 14th of December, you've got the green light to go ahead. With the Sun moving into your tenth zone of success on the 22nd of December, just before Christmas, and Jupiter also moving forward in your zone of finances, the end of 2011 should prove to be successful and crown you with success.

Karma, luck and meditation

Friends will be vitally important to your luck and success throughout 2011. You can make a great impact on others and easily gain their help and support, even financially, especially in January, with the Sun and Mars transiting your zone of friendships and life fulfilment. Simultaneously, profits will rise, with Jupiter also moving into your Sun sign.

Positive financial successes are indicated by the Sun's movement into your finance zone after the 20th of April, with Mars also conjoining Jupiter, the lucky planet, on the 1st of May. At this time some grand opportunities present themselves. There are windows of opportunities you should be more than willing to explore. These are the sorts of planetary energies that bring you extra money, the support of powerful people and even fame, if that's something you are chasing.

Your romantic luck is dependent upon favourable planets moving in your zone of love affairs and marriage, and a couple of opportunities appear, particularly when the Sun transits your fifth zone in July and Mars in September. At these points of the year, say 'yes' if you're invited on a date or have a chance to meet your soulmate.

The lucky zone of your horoscope is the ninth sign of Sagittarius, and the Sun moves into this sector on the 23rd of November. Shortly after, on the 25th, a solar eclipse has much to say about your karma; that is, what you've done in the past and what you're likely to receive as a result of those actions.

In other words, the important questions you'll need to ask yourself centre around the attitude of how you did things in the past. If you've been positive, expending your goodwill and generosity to the world around you, this latter part of 2011 will bring you some great successes, possibly unexpected luck, and certainly some additional love and friendship.

All in all, 2011 is going to be an exciting, lucky and ground-breaking year for most Aries-born individuals. Good luck, and may the stars shine on you in the coming twelve months!

ARIES

Your Bonus 2010 Three Month Forecast

OCTOBER 2010

Highlights of the month

This is a month when you can clear the backlog of all those mounds of paper—bills and other unsightly documents—that have been cluttering your house or office. Bear in mind that your external environment reflects, to a large extent, the condition of your heart and mind.

By the 5th the combined influence of Mercury and Saturn will make you more concentrated in thought and you'll be self-absorbed trying to collate, organise and reorient yourself and get your working and living environments in order.

This is also a time when you'll contemplate giving up some bad habits; for example, biting your nails, smoking, or eating your daily block of chocolate.

Contractual agreements and anything associated with loans, purchasing or selling can be dealt with throughout this month. With Mars and Venus still affecting your zone of sexuality and shared resources, there will be a desire to establish the status quo with respect to your financial commitments to the one you love.

After the 9th you can meet an exciting, stimulating person who may have an important part to play in your life. You will admire this person's individuality and it may or may not become a sexual or romantic relationship. But rest assured, when Venus and Mars affect the area of your horoscope—which they will at this time—there's no doubt you will have an instant attraction to someone you meet during this phase of your life.

The period of the 14th and up until the 23rd is a wonderful time to connect with groups of people who can help you advance in the right direction socially and spiritually. You may be attracted to joining some new organisation or association and could be surprised to meet many others who are of like mind.

This will be an interesting development in your understanding of life because you'll come to realise that your true family is not necessarily the group of people you have been born into, but more likely those you bond with and can relate to on deeper emotional, spiritual and global levels. This period of your life reveals to you a change in the direction of your interests.

From the 18th till the 20th there is an indication that travel and great joy blend to bring you an interesting journey that will further advance your inner awareness of yourself and bring your life's dream into clearer focus. You must be on guard not to overdo things because on a more practical level your immune system, blood and liver may be prone to weakness. Revisit the concept of diet and adequate exercise to keep you healthy.

Optimistic attitudes will be the medicine that helps you deal with some fragmented issues in your work life from the 22nd. You'll have the gift of the gab so don't worry if you're called into the boss's office to explain your behaviour or the behaviour of others because you'll easily win an argument or sway someone's opinion.

If your job deals with the public or you happen to be a teacher, lawyer or in some type of diplomatic arena, your large-scale projects will definitely benefit from the way you convey your ideas and plans. It appears that there may even be some influential people who are watching you at this time and your behaviour and good work will be recognised and rewarded appropriately.

Between the 27th and 31st you'll continue to express a growing interest in people of foreign cultures and one person in particular who will certainly forge a new deep and meaningful relationship with you.

Romance and friendship

On the 1st, 2nd, 5th, and 6th you'll be feeling nostalgic and also somewhat lazy. You shouldn't purchase a favour just because you can't be bothered doing the chore yourself. This puts you in an inferior position if not one of victimhood at some later stage. You may even realise that the person who is doing you a good turn is using this to their advantage.

Your intense passions and desire for someone on the 8th and 9th may not be long-lived, but boy, will it be fun! Try to learn a little more about them first. This is a very sexual couple of days.

What you discover about a friend on the 13th could be downright frustrating as you realise there is no way they're going to change to provide for your emotional needs. There's no use flogging a dead horse, so look elsewhere to fulfil your personal and romantic expectations.

Physical exercise is more important than ever between the 15th and 20th. If you find yourself cooped up, with boredom setting in, get your limbs moving and your lungs filled with fresh air. This will help you physically *and* will definitely lift your spirits to help you clear out some emotional stuff as well.

Your behaviour will be in the spotlight around the 22nd. So don't forget to polish your shoes, and your manners, for that matter. Remember that clothes do make the wo/man.

There's no disputing that, if you are brash or condescending in a social situation between the 23rd and 26th, it will go against you, especially when you don't know those who are around you very well. Be sensitive to the traditions of the situation.

You don't have to force your opinions on others on the 27th. Listen with an open mind and you'll realise that you have more in common with someone than you think.

Work and money

You will feel more in control of your financial circumstances and can achieve maximum results between the 1st and the 8th. Savings will increase if you count your pennies.

Make an extra sacrifice by putting in additional hours at work on the 14th and 15th. You may begrudge having to forfeit a couple of social events but realise this is essential to reduce your long-term stress levels.

Around the 22nd you must be careful not to run roughshod over others who are not as qualified as you. Success, power and its use or abuse will be issues that are strongly in focus. Use this power wisely, especially if you are in a position to dominate others.

A spending spree is likely on the 24th and will be lots of fun. It's not a bad idea to keep the receipts away from the prying eyes of family as they might question the amount spent!

Changes in your work routine between the 27th and 30th depend on new technical processes. These could make your job more cumbersome. You will have to work extra hard to catch up on these new systems. You believe that things should stay the same. But your boss has the last say.

Destiny dates

Positive: 1, 2, 5, 6, 8, 9, 14, 15, 16, 17, 18, 19, 20, 21, 22, 28, 29, 30, 31

Negative: 13, 24, 25, 26

Mixed: 23, 27

NOVEMBER 2010

Highlights of the month

The trend this month is to fall madly in love with someone quickly and, due to excellent communications, to also possibly involve yourself with them professionally or financially.

Between the 1st and the 5th you will feel great and your physical health will also be on an upward trend. Expect loads of vitality with a confident and optimistic view that will cause you to initiate new business plans, creative enterprises and other social strategies. This is a powerful romantic and financial cycle for you.

Speaking your mind is essential, but between the 6th and 10th you should measure your words before delivering them. There is no doubt that you will possess clarity and genuine intention but not everyone will be able to see the big picture as clearly as you do.

A constructive alliance is forecast for you from the 15th. But you need to be consistent in the way you deal with people at this time because you're likely to blow hot and cold. This alliance may be with members of your family, some friend or perhaps even a complete stranger. As I said, consistency will be the foundation of success and once you decide on your course of action you must not take 'no' for an answer. Persistence will pay off.

Be careful after the 17th when the planets Mars, Saturn and Neptune detrimentally influence your physical body. You will need to get adequate sleep and pay special attention to any medication you may be taking, as this could be the cause of diminished vitality.

The Sun enters the favourable ninth zone of travel and higher learning after the 22nd. You mustn't feel exploited by anyone at this stage but rather learn how to deal with confrontational situations in a positive manner. Someone could be thwarting your goals and your options may seem limited; but you actually have much more power in the situation than you think. This is another period of the year when self-help and educational programs will go a long way to help resolve these issues.

This month you'll be paying greater attention to your physical health and the way your fashion statements impact on those around you. Sometime around the 27th you may need to be a little careful about giving off mixed signals. Sometimes people misinterpret what your intention is and this could get you into a spot of bother. If you are conducting business, try to dress a little more conservatively because this is probably the trigger that could cause an unwanted sexual advance.

Like a bolt of lightning out of the blue, the Mars and Uranus energy around the 28th heralds some unanticipated turn of events. You may want to be somewhere else and drop everything at a moment's notice. Travel and adventure marks this time interval and you are likely to be swayed by someone who also wants to get away and have a taste of excitement. This may give you quite a great deal of enjoyment but it will also set you up for a backlog of work in your final month of the year.

Romance and friendship

Between the 3rd and 5th you are torn between varying opinions regarding a decision you must make. It's quite likely that your intuition about someone was correct from the outset. In doubting yourself you have asked others to sway your opinion. This will only serve to complicate matters. Trust your initial hunch and proceed.

On the 7th assert your true heart's desire and pursue the person you love. Don't be afraid to show your feelings. You have the blessing of Venus to receive some great, encouraging romantic responses.

If you're feeling hindered by friends on the 11th or 12th you will find it much easier to begin to communicate by sending an e-mail or voice mail and giving a big hint before speaking face to face.

Around the 14th you may decide to do something you've wanted to for a long time. You could invite a friend of like mind to join in the fun.

The planets make you determined on the 19th and 20th. Love will bring up all sorts of emotional and sexual issues for discussion. If you haven't been able to talk about these issues it's because someone has been dominating the sensual landscape. It's your turn now to fulfil your emotional needs.

There's nothing worse than thinking about what you 'could have said' in a situation. Your blood could boil over on the 22nd due to some self-righteous individual's comments. If you get an inkling someone is going to give you a hard time, you need to be quick off the mark.

Between the 28th and 30th news of a friend's misfortune will make you feel gratitude for how lucky you are. Although you will want to help them you realise their circumstances are beyond your help. Send them your best vibrations.

Work and money

Your lethargy will pass around the 7th and any physical 'dis-ease' related to your excessive work practices will also disappear. Continue to slow down and prioritise your tasks for a while.

Working on streamlining your diary is highlighted between the 9th and 13th. Spend a little time planning work effectively so you don't wear yourself into the ground.

You have the opportunity to earn more money around the 14th; however, a necessary gift, an obligatory gesture, will cost more than you expect.

You will begin to improve your lifestyle significantly by the 24th but remember this also has a great deal to do with educating yourself. It's a perfect time to enrol in a few night or correspondence courses to further your knowledge.

Speculation on the 26th is lucky for you. If you prefer the poker machine or race track it could be a timely occasion for you as well.

Between the 28th and 30th you could be overemotional about your professional duties and will not perform as well as you should. Try to see things from the other person's point of view, even if you believe you know better. Time will prove you correct.

Destiny dates

Positive: 13, 15, 24, 26

Negative: 8, 17, 19, 20, 27

Mixed: 1, 2, 3, 4, 5, 6, 7, 9, 10, 11, 12, 14, 22, 28, 29, 30

DECEMBER 2010

Highlights of the month

Blocks in relationships can resurface between the 1st and 3rd, but this is only due to you repeating certain behaviour patterns from your childhood. This year will be one in which you have gained considerable insight and, possibly by the last month of the year, you will have armed yourself with sufficient strategies for dealing with this change and not be too caught up in the trivia of day-to-day life.

You may have interest in a family business and you have a good sense of judgement at this time. From the 4th to the 6th any legal issues that have been obstructing you will go your way. The advice you receive should be taken and co-operation and teamwork will be at the heart of the good news you hear at this time.

On a romantic note you will be inspired by the one you love, or possibly someone new. Your imagination may be working overtime and this is excellent for sensual relationships and sexual pleasures. However, work could suffer so you need to be sufficiently sober to balance the practical and emotional events in the last month of 2010.

With the strong influence of Venus and Neptune in your life, you'll probably have an opportunity to be photographed and present yourself to the world in the best possible light. It's all about looking your best and being well received. You could call this a type of branding where your name and your deeds become the highlight of your life and you want to be thought of in the highest possible way.

Secrets, hidden relationships and other forms of deception and betrayal are on the cards in the last month of the year. You will need to deal with these issues; but over and above this, any form of addiction, medication or behaviour that is undermining your inner contentment should be looked at, and fairly and squarely permanently eliminated. If needs be you may need to get the appropriate counselling to get through this rather strange planetary combination.

On the 21st the final eclipse of the year is a lunar eclipse that occurs in the sign of Gemini, your zone of siblings, neighbours, mental activities, short journeys and communication. All of these issues will be prominent in your life and you will be forced, in spite of yourself, to deal with any or all of these points just mentioned.

Around the same time and for the rest of the year Mars will be moving through your zone of work and professional achievements. Being your ruling planet this is a remarkable planetary transit that represents the continuous work and planning of 2010 that will pay off, if not earlier, then certainly in the closing chapter of 2010.

Not only will you experience greater self-esteem and professional upliftment, but your finances should also be in better shape.

Leading up to Christmas Jupiter promises to make this festive season one of the most expensive you've had but that won't bother you because you are feeling quite in tune with the pleasure of giving and benefiting others. The final tone of the year is one of tremendous energy, physical vitality and busyness. It appears that you'll have a rich and fulfilling Christmas with many beautiful friends to surround you.

The position of Venus around the last week of the month represents, along with Uranus, an attraction to many different people from all walks of life. This will be an active and enjoyable festive period and the indications are that this will carry over through the holiday period and on into the new year.

When all is said and done, 2010 should be a fruitful and fulfilling year.

Romance and friendship

You could feel as if you are being outshone by a friend in some social situation on the 1st and 2nd. Get behind them and do everything you can to graciously help them attain the best for themselves. You'll be surprised at the accolades you receive in return for your aid.

On the 6th you'll get caught up in the excitement of a new domestic situation in which everyone is celebrating some event together. The aftermath, however, will reveal that the responsibility of certain individuals has been conveniently sidestepped. Clarify the terms beforehand.

In your desire to do something extraordinary you might go a little bit too far between the 8th and 14th. This might give you some short-term satisfaction but stop and think about the long-term ramifications of your actions on others in your life.

Be gentle in pointing out the past transgressions of someone close to you on the 18th. You may be totally unaware of just how painful the topic of discussion is to them. Forget your purely intellectual perspective and employ compassion.

You'll be embarrassed into making a donation around the 23rd. This will go against your better judgement. To save face and keep your ego intact, you'll act in a manner contrary to what your heart is telling you. Don't live up to others' expectations. Live by your own standards.

Work on health issues around the 24th and 25th. You need to muster up as much energy as possible for the Christmas break. Increase your vitamin intake and eat healthier foods at the Christmas feast.

If you feel flat in your love life between the 27th and 31st, make a deal with your partner to spend time alone without friends or relatives in the picture. This will make the last days of 2010 so much more satisfying.

Work and money

You are particularly sensitive and irritable over financial matters on the 3rd. Others won't understand where you are coming from. If you can't get people to identify with your ideas, postpone discussions that might simply go round and round in circles.

Between the 7th and 14th step up to the plate and show what you're really made of. If you're reluctant to take the lead and express different views, rest assured you'll receive 100 per cent support from others—even those who would previously have opposed your suggestions.

You mustn't become dejected if a financial plan doesn't work out exactly the way you anticipate between the 15th and the 18th. Have a couple more irons in the fire so that when and if something does bomb out you'll still have another plan to pursue. There are bright new opportunities in the closing weeks of the year.

Between the 20th and 24th, dare to question the motives of a person you work with and reveal important information because they may not be quite as dependable as you think they are.

Opening your mouth could fuel rumours on the 29th. Silence is golden and work will flourish by saying as little as possible. Less is more!

Destiny dates

Positive: 4, 5, 7

Negative: 1, 2, 3, 15, 16, 17, 20, 22, 23, 27, 28, 29, 30, 31

Mixed: 6, 8, 9, 10, 11, 12, 13, 14, 18, 21, 24, 25

ARIES

2011:
Month by Month Predictions

JANUARY 2011

He who is not courageous enough to take risks will accomplish nothing in life.

—Muhammad Ali

Highlights of the month

You mustn't let a sense of oppression or restriction mar the first month of 2011 for you. With Saturn transiting your zone of interpersonal relationships, it's quite likely that little things will cause you to react intensely and this will be predominant between the 1st and the 5th. Find an adequate outlet to express these feelings, otherwise you may feel cut off or confined as a result.

Your relationships are likely to be 'under a cloud' at this time and the challenging relationship between Venus and Neptune is not going to make matters any better. You need to be clear, concise and honest in your dealings with others and tell them exactly how you feel.

Bottling up your feelings will only make you feel

more depleted at this time and, between the 7th and the 11th, you could feel as if your partner or significant other is punishing you for simply being yourself.

Things lighten up after the 14th when the Sun conjoins your zone of social engagements, friends and mutually supportive networks. This can be a time of fun, of putting aside your personal concerns and making an opportunity to reignite the enthusiasm that is so very much a part of your Aries nature.

You receive an increased lift in spirits as a result of Venus and its favourable influence on your Sun sign after the 17th. Mercury also gives you a knack of saying the right thing at the right time after the 21st. You'll be reorienting yourself towards your business and commercial activities and work will be a priority.

You should make hay while the sun shines because this is an excellent opportunity to create an impact on your employers and other people with whom you do business.

You'll be thinking of the past towards the latter part of the month. Unfortunately, you may be worried about something you've said or done and this could momentarily distract you from more important matters. Try to keep your mind on the job and venture to sort out these problems of yesteryear only during your spare time.

Saturn has a marked influence on the life of Aries-born people throughout the whole of 2011. In particular, during its retrograde movement after the 26th, relationship matters could come to the fore. A greater sense of responsibility will be evident at this time, but communication may not flow so easily.

A difficult period is forecast between the 28th and the 30th; however, at that time, you can make some significant breakthroughs when Venus and Mercury bring you some better fortune in respect of romance, personal relationships and domestic life.

Romance and friendship

You need to get cracking on a whole new romantic strategy on the 3rd, particularly if you feel as if your relationship is a one-way street. You have to earn respect, so don't be afraid to speak out and tell others exactly what you want.

Between the 8th and the 11th, wrecked routines at home will create havoc because you don't feel as though you have the support of other members of the family. Be bold enough to come up with alternative ways to delegate work at home.

Friends are unreliable around the 16th due to the presence of Mars in your zone of friendships. In fact you may end up having a head-to-head with someone who just doesn't want to listen to your opinions. Try to be more accommodating because you have a somewhat larger ego around this time.

On the 18th you'll feel like a 'cosmic tourist' with your partner or friend making you feel as if you're living in a bubble. You don't seem to be able to make any connection with them, but things should pick up by the 20th.

You will feel somewhat restricted by others in your social life around the 22nd. If friends are leaning on you and demanding too much of your time, you have to know when to say 'no'.

Financial matters, shared resources and other issues surrounding money, debts and loans could be a cause of problems between you and a close member of your family. Don't let money get in the road of your personal relationships from the 23rd to the 25th.

If you've had someone on your restriction list, the 30th is a good time for a heart-to-heart with them. Your love and tenderness will be strong and you can expect your partner to reciprocate.

Work and money

Short journeys, travels for work-related matters and generally not being on time are likely between the 1st and the 4th. Try to plan your appointments so that you don't need to double up on travelling distances and *expenses*.

You're off to a flying start, with great ideas and good energy—much of which you can share with your co-workers—between the 3rd and the 6th. Try to get others onside who think like you and you will augment the power of your concepts. You will accomplish good results as a team.

Educational pursuits need to complement both your business and your personal life, so taking on a new course of learning is quite likely between the 12th and the 16th. Try your hand at something new because this will improve your skills in the very job you happen to be in right now.

Unreliable co-workers could cause problems with your timetable between the 22nd and the 26th. Make sure you get confirmation of appointments before you turn up.

A workplace romance or at least social activities that involve people you work with in life bring considerable happiness and satisfaction to you on the 30th and the 31st. This is a time to network and share your resources.

Destiny dates

Positive: 6, 12, 13, 14, 15, 17, 20, 21, 31

Negative: 7, 8, 9, 10, 11, 18, 22, 23, 24, 25, 26, 27, 28, 29

Mixed: 1, 2, 3, 4, 5, 16, 19, 30

FEBRUARY 2011

Highlights of the month

You're likely to want to get things done quickly—might I say in too much of a hurry for your own good, perhaps—throughout February. This is on account of Venus and Uranus being in a difficult aspect, particularly from the 2nd.

You need to curb your impulses, especially if you've been disillusioned with relationships and some new opportunity presents itself. You want distraction; this could come in the form of a temptation or something you ordinarily wouldn't think of doing. Try to exercise some consideration for other people's feelings in the first week of the month.

During this cycle, Jupiter enters your Sun sign and makes you bold and confident, so much so that you're likely to discard conventions and investigate new ways of thinking and living. You want to be more self-sufficient and prove you're independent enough to achieve your objectives in life, but it's wise not to overstep the mark.

Between the 6th and the 13th, your personality is excessive and you're likely to say and do things that you may regret. Exercising self-restraint and being more resourceful through adapting yourself to the circumstances of the moment is the way forward.

When the Sun moves to the low-key zone of your horoscope on the 14th, this self-control that I talk about may arise more naturally for you, without any effort on your part. You'll see the sense in pulling back and not using force to achieve your desires.

Throughout February, most of the planets occupy the upper part of your horoscope. Success, making money and being received well by the general public will be important components in the motivation for most of what you do.

After the 20th, however, you must be careful not to rub people up the wrong way because Mercury with Mars will make you prone to be outspoken, insensitive and probably even callous in the way you deal with others. Try to sweeten your words because this will return back to you with good interest. There are some hindrances between the 21st and the 24th.

The combined influence of Mars and Neptune are notorious for causing allergic reactions, physical obstructions and maybe even minor medical issues, and this can occur in the last week of the month. Make your body strong leading up to this date. Exercise well, get adequate rest and take special care with your diet by not overdoing certain types of food and especially alcohol.

Venus moving to your eleventh house of friendship and love can bring a lovely touch of attractiveness and social intercourse your way from the 26th to the 28th.

Romance and friendship

Communication is great on the 2nd and you can make friends and share new ideas with a new group of people. Interesting encounters and an alignment with those of similar ideas and aspirations take place due to the new Moon in your zone of social affairs on the 3rd.

On the 4th and 5th you may be impulsive and have a tendency to do things that could put you at odds with your peer group. Also, try to maintain an element of privacy, especially if sexual affairs are on your mind.

You're physically strong and need a lot of outdoor activity rather than staying indoors around the 6th. Engage your partner or friends to get out with you on a run or go to the gym and work-out. This will help you find an adequate outlet for your energies. This could also be a time of disagreement.

Home affairs are spotlighted between the 14th and the 19th. Lay low and spend quality time with your nearest and dearest. An old friend whom you haven't heard from in a while could make a show and this could also add a touch of joy to your family circle.

You could be drawn or attracted to a talented jerk around the 20th. Irrespective of what others say, you have to trust your heart and make your own decisions. Underneath, this person may simply be insecure and here could be an opportunity to help someone find their way clear of their past.

You are persuasive between the 22nd and the 25th. You may be able to speak to the group, mediate between two parties who are having difficulties, and come out feeling good about yourself. This cycle brings with it renewed self-respect and a certain position within your social group.

Your sense of self is strong on the 27th, so don't be afraid to ask for what you want.

Work and money

You stand out from your peers at work by the 4th, but also have the opportunity to lead others towards integrity. It's a rigorous routine up until the 9th and you may have to be hard on those who were previously friends but are now subordinates.

You seek new skills and a high standard from yourself and this could make others feel a little less capable than you. On the 18th, the full Moon taking place in your zone of health and work practices, means newly emerging systems of work and efficiency will occupy your mind. On the 19th and 20th you need to encourage others to do their best without making them feel inadequate.

Financial matters and expenditures are strongly highlighted between the 22nd and the 24th. Working through your finances and establishing a new budget could be in order. You need to get others onboard, otherwise you'll be travelling this path alone. You need the support of your peers and family members to make this work.

Communication will be highlighted between the 25th and the 27th. Your writing skills, the way you present your ideas and your overall strategy need to be clear and concise so that others can understand you.

Destiny dates

Positive: 14, 15, 16, 17, 18, 19, 25, 26, 27, 28

Negative: 5, 7, 8, 10, 11, 12, 13, 21

Mixed: 2, 4, 6, 9, 20, 22, 23, 24

MARCH 2011

Highlights of the month

Abundance is your key word throughout March and it seems as if the lucky planet Jupiter is prepared to bring you many opportunities for wealth and friendship at this time of the year.

Once in twelve years, Jupiter makes contact with your Sun sign. This indicates an extraordinarily uplifting time for you, where new windows of opportunity should be sought and acted upon. The difficult influence of Saturn in your relationship zone is considerably softened by Jupiter's presence here, and I can safely say that, whatever problems many Arians might have been experiencing so far will be easier to bear, at least for the rest of 2011.

From the 6th, you can attempt a new form of communication with your friends and lovers and you'll be surprised at the positive response you receive when doing so. If the current techniques you've been using to communicate aren't working for you, there's no point continuing with them, is there?

You have a greater sense of spiritual connectedness this month and, believe it or not, this may also be one of the factors that is providing you with much more luck. Significant dates in March include the 10th, 15th and the 19th.

In the first two weeks of the month, take careful note of the peak energies around at these times because important turning points in your life could be occurring. In particular, the Sun at right angles to your karmic planets will indicate significant changes in your domestic sphere and attitudes to your parents, siblings and other relatives.

A dose of electric energy will kick-start your activities after the 21st if you've relaxed into complacent lethargy. The Sun will revitalise you and Uranus will make you much more progressive and willing to try new things. You can expect a whole new swag of friends and workplace opportunities arising and coming your way after this.

Expenditure and/or income matters are high on your agenda from the 27th until the 30th. Finding new ways to cut back on spending yet maintaining a high-quality lifestyle requires a creative touch on your part. Don't be afraid to listen to what family members have to offer in this respect. Keep your mind open to see the sense and value of what's being offered.

You may oscillate between moments of ecstasy and the pits of despair between the 29th and the 31st, and this is because of the tough aspect between Jupiter and Saturn. Try to weather the storms of life with an even mind at this time, and don't scatter your energies in too many directions. I suggest you remain quiet because this will help you transition into the next month.

Romance and friendship

Love is in the air! The Moon connects with Venus on the 1st, and its loving vibrations continue up until the 4th. The new Moon also occurs on the 4th, in one of your most spiritual sectors, indicating your connection to the cosmic forces of nature. You'll be interested in issues of karma.

You may be demanding of others' attention around the 5th, so try to use a little persuasiveness and charm if affection is what you desire. You can't squeeze blood out of a stone, as they say, but a soft approach might create a similar miracle for you, emotionally speaking.

You feel as if someone is keeping secrets from you between the 6th and the 8th. Each person is entitled to a sacrosanct space for themselves, but this could be bothering you and you need to talk about it. If the other party isn't prepared to open up and share their feelings with you, you'll just have to bite the bullet and live with it for the moment.

You're amorous on the 16th, 20th and 21st because new opportunities for love and romance present themselves to you. Sexual connections are hot on the 22nd. Take full advantage of these sizzling planetary energies. This is a time when you are likely to be risky in your romantic adventures but will enjoy every minute of it.

Time off is recommended between the 27th and the 30th as Venus enters your quiet zone of relaxation. It's not a bad idea to take a short holiday, a calm weekend away with your loved one, and simply chill out.

Social engagements bubble over in the last few days of the month, so try to get enough sleep to be able to enjoy the fun fully. You may be burning the midnight oil around the 31st.

Work and money

You could feel some frustration between the 1st and the 5th. You are charming and want to connect with the group but feel that there is a subversive undercurrent of activity occurring, including rumours and other malicious innuendo. Keep your nose to the grindstone and don't get involved in this stuff.

You are precise in the way you approach your work between the 7th and the 9th. You may uncover things that others have left undone. You need to bring these matters to the attention of the appropriate people because this will streamline your work.

Take precautions with your health leading up to the 19th as the full Moon revisits your zone of health. If you're careful with your diet, you'll be able to improve your vitality overall and come out feeling wonderful for the coming weeks.

On the 20th there are new business opportunities, public relations exercises and negotiations happening in which you can be a key player. Make your point decisively and win over the other side.

Work peaks for you between the 24th and the 28th, with a coveted position placed in your hands if you so choose. Financial remuneration is also on the cards after the 30th. If money has been sparse for you up to now, you can look forward to a little extra at the end of March.

Destiny dates

Positive: 9, 10, 15, 16, 20, 21, 22, 24, 25, 26

Negative: Nil

Mixed: 1, 2, 3, 4, 5, 6, 7, 8, 19, 27, 28, 29, 30, 31

APRIL 2011

Highlights of the month

Things may appear to be at a standstill this month, at least in the opening phase. But, do you know what? Nothing is ever completely at a standstill, as Albert Einstein figured out when he wrote his theory of relativity. Everything is constantly in motion, and what appears to be a stalemate—some type of stagnation—is really an opportunity for you to look forward to see how you can best make the most of what you have.

Mars and Uranus combine their forces to bring you some immense challenges after the 4th. Nuisances, coupled with pent-up energy, are likely to cause you to explode. It's best not to take on additional responsibilities, and this is where a so-called 'standstill' may possibly work to your benefit far more than you could ever imagine.

Transits like this one can cause you to be wasteful, excessive, speculative and maybe even dangerous to yourself and others. Restrain your speech and listen to the still, inner voice deep within you for guidance.

You have an influential touch, an ability to sway others after the 12th, and you must use your powers of speech and intelligence in the best possible way. You can come to the assistance of a friend and must not withhold information or good advice. By sharing these spiritual resources percolating within you, you'll gain a great deal of satisfaction by helping others through the dark nights of their soul.

Whereas you'll be helping others up until the 14th, a new development takes place for you sometime around the middle of the month; in particular, after the 16th, when Venus enters your Sun sign. Venus's presence will act like a floodlight of energy, bringing with it greater popularity, a renewed interest in your social affairs and shared obligations.

You'll be more sensitive to what's happening around you and will also probably lavish some money on yourself by purchasing some new clothes, accessories or even gadgets just to keep up with the Jones's. If it doesn't break the budget, I say: 'So what!' Enjoy yourself, feel good and share a bit of that goodwill around.

Take care between the 19th and the 22nd. Mars opposes Saturn, Mercury conjoins Mars, along with Venus conjoining Uranus. These planetary combinations act in a way to cause mishaps and other problems in your life. If you're operating machinery or dealing with electrical devices, exercise care and don't shortcut any safety measures. Pay more attention to your environment and what's happening around you, especially if you're responsible for other people, including young ones.

The month peaks with Venus and Uranus in aspect to the Sun, bringing a jolt of excitement to your life. Meeting someone new is always fun and can restore faith in your self-confidence. Take full advantage of the positive romantic vibrations that you'll feel at the end of April.

Romance and friendship

With Mars activating your personal life and in particular your relationships from the 2nd, you can expect things to heat up in the emotional department. Your partner or spouse may be demanding too much, especially if you have extra work on your plate. You are keen to show the world what you're made of and the new Moon sets the trend for a 'retrofit' of your personality and general approach to life on the 3rd.

Balancing your affairs will be one of the key issues between the 4th and the 10th. Responsibilities at home may be at odds with your hectic lifestyle, and some troubles around the 11th could throw a spanner in the works if you are trying to mend a rift with a loved one.

Children feature strongly in your life between the 12th and the 16th. If you are a parent who is working and not able to spend as much time as you would like with your young ones, this is the time to make an extra effort to cement the family unit.

The new Moon's energies that occurred earlier in the month will continue in greater force on the 18th. The full Moon, which occupies your eighth zone of personal transformation, drives you deeper into yourself to understand the reasons why you are who you are.

Love is also hot for singles from the 19th to the 22nd. Hopefully you'll be out and about flaunting your best personality traits if you're trying to find love at this time. Journeys for social reasons from the 21st to the 25th also give you an opportunity to meet new types of people. Communication is much more rewarding after the 23rd, when Mercury goes direct.

When Venus comes to your Sun sign on the 21st, you'll feel an uplifting of your emotional and social needs. You may also want to beautify yourself by trying new fashions, fabrics and even hairstyles that are normally not 'you'. Experimentation is the only way you will understand others' reactions to your new look, particularly between the 26th and 30th.

Work and money

You are keen to get all of your work done throughout April, which is shown by the presence of Mars moving through your Sun sign. From the 2nd to the 4th you'll be a dynamo of energy and can achieve a considerable amount on your own. If you need to work with others, however, you could feel stifled by what you consider to be lack of initiative on their part. You must be more respectful of others and how they approach their work.

Your money focus is tied up with real estate, fixed assets and other investments that may be used to smarten up your home and living circumstances between the 5th and the 10th. Buying and selling property could also be part of your agenda this month.

Expenditures are high after the 20th, when the position of the Sun indicates you'll be burning a hole in your pocket. You are earning well but spending just as much. The Moon comes to your rescue after the 23rd until the 25th. Some unforeseen cash could come to light, pulling you out of a financial ditch.

Destiny dates

Positive: 9, 10, 12, 13, 14, 15, 16, 18, 23, 28, 29, 30

Negative: Nil

Mixed: 1, 2, 3, 4, 5, 6, 7, 8, 11, 17, 19, 20, 21, 22, 24, 25, 26, 27

MAY 2011

Highlights of the month

At this time you might feel a strong sense of separation, of pulling apart and feeling isolated in your personal relationships and, if you happen to be married, the pressure may be even greater.

Although deep within you, you understand that everything in this world is impermanent, including relationships, you need not throw out the baby with the bathwater just yet.

With Venus and Saturn challenging you to handle the humdrum aspects of life and love, you may opt to try something completely different and to throw in the towel, so to speak. However, I suggest you hang in there just a little bit longer, to see just how much deeper you can dig for love in your effort to attain a more selfless state in your relationships. Of course, this won't be easy, but your rewards could be well worth it.

Mars entering your finance zone after the 3rd is both problematic and encouraging for your income at the same time. On the one hand, you'll make greater efforts to increase your earning capacity, but may also find the spendthrift within you coming on very strong.

Try to keep tabs on where you're spending your money so you can create a better budget that will allow you to enjoy the things in life that you value. By the same token, between the 4th and the 8th, disputes over financial priorities may arise, both in your personal life and on the work front. Your value system will be at odds with someone else's and so the operative word will be 'compromise'.

Jupiter creates some wonderful new opportunities in your workplace after the 10th, and this is augmented by Mercury's conjunction with Venus. You may finally decide to forge ahead on your own in work. Setting up a new business, branding yourself more effectively and connecting with the community and new business markets are all likely effects of these planetary influences.

Coincidentally, Venus and Mercury lend their energy to your karmic basket from the 11th. The result is that, after the 12th, you're likely to see an improvement in your cash position from an increase in pay or additional bonuses you had not expected to come to the surface. Just don't spend too freely, as I said earlier. This will be a test of your ability to monitor and discipline yourself financially.

The Sun highlights your need to travel, to get mobile, enjoy new sights and hear new sounds after the 15th. You're keen to travel and venture into unknown territories, meet new people and expand your mind. This is therefore a great time to make new acquaintances but also to consider how you can explore your mental horizons and even take on some form of interesting study.

Your identity is changing and, when the Sun makes any sort of contact with Neptune, as it will on the 22nd, you may reach a point in your thinking where what you feel about yourself is not adequate. Generally you may be confused about your role in society, or the world or your destiny.

You need to utilise your intuitive powers to gain answers, because what you read or hear from others may not satisfy your soul's yearnings. Trust yourself and just be yourself, as this is the safest way to find happiness in your life.

Additionally, you have good financial and professional prospects between the 23rd and the 26th. Move ahead fearlessly and don't be afraid of change.

Romance and friendship

You want something new and alive in your relationships on the 3rd due to the new Moon. You will compare your current relationship with that of someone else who appears to have a better rapport with their partner than you do. Be satisfied and patient with what you have up until the 5th, when romance takes a turn for the better.

You can 'let the good times roll' after the 10th. Mercury and Venus give you a wonderful blend of optimism, humour and charm, making you the life of the party. Just be careful you don't bite off more than you can chew because engagements, invitations and offers of love and romance will be plentiful.

Love is also spotlighted between the 14th and the 16th. You must encourage the person you love to be more in tune with what you want; what your dreams are. Otherwise, how are they going to know? It's up to you to communicate your feelings in terms they can understand.

A new circle of friends from the 22nd could create some embarrassment for your partner or another friend if they don't feel comfortable or are not familiar with these people. Make sure you take time on the introductions, and try to act as a mediator by highlighting the similarities between them rather than their differences.

Between the 24th and the 27th, make sure you look at the motives of someone who may be advising you, supposedly in your best interest, but who could possibly have some other reason for being nice. All that glitters is not gold.

Try to keep your personal affairs private around the 31st. E-mail correspondence in particular should be for your eyes only. If you share some of your secrets, it could get back to another person and create problems for you.

Work and money

The new Moon in Taurus is excellent for striking up new deals, coming up with new ideas in your work and generally communicating and sharing your values on a new project. You can create a happy state of mind with all concerned between the 3rd and the 10th.

By the 11th, when Mars enters your zone of finances and income, you may be hard at it but also possibly pushing your concepts and methodologies down someone else's throat. This can result in retaliatory action, so temper your ideas, no matter how enthusiastic you feel.

It might be time to give your co-workers a bit of a shock by giving them a taste of something new between the 21st and the 27th. If you're in a position of authority, you need to mix it up—keep it interesting—to generate some excitement in the workplace. This will definitely tell on people's productivity.

Don't let inattentiveness create disagreement over contracts on the 31st. Someone may choose to renegotiate and it could be a difficult task getting to the bottom of why this has happened. It's likely you haven't paid enough attention to the detail and, as they say, that's where the 'devil' can be found.

Destiny dates

Positive: 9, 10, 12, 14, 15, 16, 21, 23

Negative: Nil

Mixed: 3, 4, 5, 6, 7, 8, 11, 22, 24, 25, 26, 27, 31

JUNE 2011

Highlights of the month

You sense your power, your abilities and your capacity to achieve great success in June. Fortunately, the Sun now creates a favourable aspect with Saturn and, from the 1st, you'll feel more capable of concentrating on your objectives.

Planning effectively for the future will be high on your agenda and will underpin the success of your action in the next two or three months. Note also that a solar eclipse in your zone of money and income will bring you to a higher level of understanding of these things.

Such great self-confidence brings with it a perception of your strength of character and dignity and, in your social affairs, you have the power to influence others and change the course of your life.

Leadership opportunities prevail and you should throw your hat in the ring if an offer of some new and coveted position is mentioned. Mercury makes you deliberate, clear and persuasive in your arguments between the 8th and the 13th. If, for example, you were to go for a new job or seek a better position with the organisation you're currently in, you can be quite successful. This rests predominantly on your high level of self-confidence and the power that you now exude.

Your domestic affairs will spotlight your need to turn away from external matters between the 14th and the 16th, on which date a lunar eclipse takes place. Try to stay indoors and deal with those hidden matters that may be eating away at you if they remain unresolved. By getting rid of these issues, you'll be in a better position to focus your energies on alternatives that can bring you lasting fulfilment.

Excellent transits from Mercury and Venus to Neptune and Saturn on the 17th and 18th mean that you can mould your ideas in a practical way and achieve some steady results. Your brilliant thinking will convince others of the merits of your ideas and your work should be a satisfying arena of activity up until the 21st.

Try not to argue with your boss or other managers between the 22nd and the 26th. You may have ideas about how you want things to be but may not be completely aware of the bigger picture. Sometimes it's best to concede that you don't know everything. Entertainment, fun and social relaxation mark the close of June and, from the 29th onwards, Venus and Mercury add further benefits to your life.

Romance and friendship

Both the solar and the lunar eclipses in June make this an important time for your relationships. You need to use new methods of communication, particularly from the 1st to the 8th. Mercury makes you capable of both listening and speaking in equal measure, which is really the hallmark of a great communicator.

On the 10th, Venus transits your third zone of communications and travels. Perhaps the best way to reconnect with a loved one or friend is to take time out and go somewhere special together.

The period of the 12th to the 16th, during which a lunar eclipse takes place, may bring many emotional upheavals, including jealousy. If you're entering a new relationship, you need to accommodate each other and accept that some transition is necessary. Therefore, don't deny the other person their past.

Mercury moving through your zone of family and domestic issues after the 17th means that you and your family should be working together on shared ideas to make your home life smoother. If you have an unruly child, you'll need to employ original methods to get them to respect your command. The best way to do this is with the incentive of rewards rather than fear of punishment.

Friends are too forthcoming between the 18th and the 23rd, and their opinions may not be welcome. Sometimes honesty is hard to take and, if someone you usually trust doesn't approve of your behaviour or course of action, you'll disagree.

Between the 28th and the 30th, slabs of conversation you're having with someone evaporate because you have other things on your mind. Make sure to ask others to repeat themselves, especially if the conversation centres on topics involving deeper emotional issues.

Work and money

Any plan you have needs careful execution between the 3rd and the 5th when Mercury, in hard aspect to Neptune, influences you, along with Jupiter transiting your zone of finance. Certainly, these ideas are great but you may be confused about how to implement them.

Sometime around the 8th to the 13th, rely on the wisdom, experience and friendship of an older, more stable individual. This could be an employer who regards you highly and is prepared to help you through the maze of confusion just now.

You could realise that you've had blinkers on after the 14th and have been completely overlooking an area of business that could enhance your bank balance. Communicate—or at least make an effort after the 16th—to forge ahead in some unchartered waters. This will yield some great financial results in the coming months.

There's no point beating around the bush after the 22nd. Stake your claim and put forward your ideas boldly, otherwise you won't get your desired responses. Wait for your creative seeds to take root in the minds of those to whom you've presented them.

On the 29th, an error could turn out to be a blessing in disguise.

Destiny dates

Positive: 1, 2, 6, 7, 8, 9, 10, 11

Negative: 19, 20, 23, 24, 25, 26

Mixed: 3, 4, 5, 12, 13, 14, 15, 16, 17, 18, 21, 22, 28, 29, 30

JULY 2011

Highlights of the month

A gentle approach is what is needed throughout July, especially if you're dealing with people who are difficult. The Sun and its influence on you is significant this month. There are aspects, particularly relating to Saturn and your Sun sign, which show you're likely to be impatient with those who are slower to grasp things.

An important axiom by which you can improve matters this month has to do with the idea that others are more likely to follow your lead by your example rather than your words. Test this out and see what happens. I think when you put this to the test, you'll see that others are more likely to want to support you because they see that your confidence, coupled with your accommodating attitude, makes you more likeable and therefore more valued.

You're able to take much of the previous month's frustration and anger and channel that very well after the 6th. Reason? Mars' and Saturn's influence on your marital sector—the public relations zone of your horoscope—is working very well this month, showing that you can achieve things through extended concentration. A useful key word for you at this time would be 'constructiveness'. You need to be practical, creative and accommodating, and wrap all that up in a good plan.

When the Sun moves to your zone of entertainment, sports and creative enterprise on the 17th, you'll feel fulfilled, knowing that much of your work is now paying off. This is also an excellent time to reconnect with your child within.

Try to enjoy the things you did as a youth by paying more attention to youngsters, especially if you're a parent. Having fun, telling a joke and getting out and exploring what's available artistically and creatively will make you feel younger.

An important transit of Mercury after the 20th requires you to rethink some of your workplace practices. Mercury is very analytical and therefore you will be rethinking some of your attitudes and processes. This is great because it will make you more efficient, which in turn will free you up to do more fun things. Incidentally, this efficiency will sit well with your employers. You can be more productive as a result.

You may have what you consider to be some brilliant ideas between the 28th and 30th, but Neptune's opposition to Mercury means that you may not have all your facts and figures straight. It's best to postpone them until you gain some greater clarity.

Romance and friendship

They say that 'home is where the heart is' and there's no doubt the new Moon in the sign of Cancer, your zone of inner contentment, will play a large part in determining your romantic affairs this month. You'll learn very quickly that you need to be happy in yourself, you can't expect others to fill that gap. Try to develop some creative outlets on the 3rd, when the Moon transits your zone of creativity and entertainment.

From the 4th to the 7th, Venus activates your zone of family. An older relative could visit, or you may have the opportunity to revisit one of your old stomping grounds from childhood. School reunions are also possible after the 11th.

There's a full Moon in Capricorn on the 15th. Your emotions should be warm, endearing and this will make you popular, especially up until the 21st. Make yourself available if friends are asking you to be part of their activities, even if you feel a little low-key on the 16th.

By the 28th, you could feel somewhat lethargic, even lazy, in love, and might be expecting others to fulfil you. Remember, love is a two-way street and, if you're making your demands unreasonable, others might be disinclined to give you anything much at all.

One thing, however. Up until the 30th, your

laziness, as I call it, could give you a spark of creative brilliance, which can be utilised to stimulate new ideas and conversation between you and others.

You may still be somewhat intense by the 31st, but well-timed communication can create plenty of breathing space for both of you. Remember, even if you're not physically together, too many text messages, phone calls or e-mails may still make the other person feel like you're smothering them. Back off a little.

Work and money

You are innovative this month because of the presence of Uranus in your Sun sign. This will continue for sometime but the tension of Saturn, the traditional planet, can't be underestimated. Balance the old with the new, professionally speaking. In particular, the 7th, 9th and 14th will be stressful and could cause you to be extreme.

Be careful with your appointments from the 15th to the 24th. Don't leave anything to chance. Be logical when you speak so that you can make a greater impact on others. Prepare your notes beforehand and research your topic so you are able to give the appropriate answers when important questions are directed at you.

You need to request the help of a friend with whom you have worked previously. Their expertise will be invaluable to you at this time and they have some unique perspectives that will most certainly enhance your proposals and business negotiation skills.

Try not to be too clinical in the way you do your work this month. Employ a little bit of fun, especially after the 29th, and utilise the energies of Venus to doll up your proposals, your ideas and business meetings. A little bit of fun can decompress the tension and get people onside.

Destiny dates

Positive: 3, 4, 5, 6, 11, 29, 31

Negative: 9, 14

Mixed: 7, 15, 16, 17, 18, 19, 21, 22, 23, 24, 28, 30

AUGUST 2011

Highlights of the month

You mustn't allow your mind to trick you into believing that being cautious is in some way expressing doubt or a lack of self-confidence. Uncertainty is part and parcel of everyone's journey at different times. You may feel as if you're not up to the task during the first few days of the month, but after the 4th, optimistic Jupiter will definitely spur you on to move forward in your plans.

Mercury is retrograde and continues to create contractual or communication difficulties for you this month. You must therefore be on guard not to skip pertinent points in communication and most definitely read between the lines or you'll be misguided.

Indecision, inattentiveness and a lack of clear thinking characterises the period of the 8th until the 11th. Be especially careful of people who try to sell you what you don't need or who convince you that you're not as good as you are. You need to continue to develop self-confidence and insight to deal with unusual characters who throw up lies just now.

Health concerns underscore some of your problems during August, and it's well known that the body and the mind are connected. During Venus's transit after the 17th, you may feel a little low-key and unable to perform at your optimum. Again, this could be part of the reason why you don't feel quite capable enough. But this will soon pass and, around the 19th, you should feel a burst of life and energy again, giving you a much needed boost of confidence.

Don't burn the candle at both ends after the 22nd. Mars may make you hot-headed and, if you've been unable to complete some of your chores, you'll be over-compensating in trying to catch up.

Mars's entry into your zone of family and domestic issues stirs up trouble on the home front. You need to understand that by keeping balanced yourself, you will assist others to do the same. Don't stir up trouble where it's not necessary and, better still, bite your tongue, even if you feel as though you're completely and 100 per cent correct on any point. Keeping the peace will be more important than being right.

You could be quite seductive in the last week of the month, particularly when the Sun and Neptune influence you very powerfully. The only problem is that you may be misguided about whom you're showering your affections on. Take a step back and give people a second glance before you put all your eggs in one basket, romantically speaking.

Romance and friendship

This is one of the more positive and exciting months of the year as far as love is concerned, with the Sun and Venus both activating your zone of love affairs.

With Saturn continuing to hammer your relationships, this is a welcome relief, but you'll still need to express fully how you feel between the 5th and the full Moon of the 13th. This week could be a long one; the less you repress your feelings and the more you tell it how it is, the more likely you're able to move forward in your love life.

On the 14th, someone will be playing cat and mouse with you. If you run after them, you'll demean yourself, lower your values and not feel at all good about it. The cycle between the 15th and the 17th is all about re-establishing your values and not selling yourself short.

You're cautioned when Venus enters your zone of health and vitality on the 22nd. Express yourself fully because holding back will create damaging energies that will impact upon your wellbeing. Remain acutely aware of this, especially up until the 24th, when the Sun also brings with it a greater degree of awareness of these issues.

Between the 25th and the 27th, the issue of commitment may need to be discussed. Mars, in a very tough response to Saturn, may cause passive aggression to dominate your affairs.

On the 29th, with Venus casting a favourable influence to your tenth zone of ego and self-awareness, these matters can be resolved favourably. But you mustn't continue to hold grudges by making any superficial peace treaties.

Work and money

Abrupt timing schedules or changes in people's plans can send you off balance this month, so it's important to have a careful, steady approach to your work. Take some time on the 3rd and the 4th to pull back the reins and discipline yourself and others so that clear goals can be met.

Don't allow hidden agendas to railroad you after the 10th. Ask questions and get to the bottom of a situation if your intuition tells you that things don't feel right. Someone could be playing you and trying to take advantage of the situation for their own personal gains.

Tact and diplomacy are essential to further your business and career interests between the 14th and the 18th. Even if someone else is blunt in demanding something of you, you mustn't ruin your reputation by lowering yourself to their standards.

Some wonderful financial opportunities can spur you on to bigger and better things from the 19th to the 27th. The influence of Jupiter becomes stronger and you have the determination to make your dreams come true. Take adequate rest after the 29th because your energies could be on the wane. You need to remain strong for the upcoming workload because it looks like it may be getting more intense.

Destiny dates

Positive: 3, 4, 15, 16, 18, 19, 20, 21, 23, 24

Negative: 5, 6, 7, 8, 9, 10, 11, 12, 13

Mixed: 14, 17, 22, 25, 26, 27, 29

SEPTEMBER 2011

Highlights of the month

Things may be moving far too slowly for your liking throughout September, which is why patience and endurance are necessary as key characteristics of your personality just now. You must persevere, even if things could be going against you.

The 2nd and the 3rd should give you enough confidence to feel as if something in your work is going right. The Sun is an excellent bolster to your workplace activities and Mercury also brings with it some good news, letters or e-mails that promise better times, if not better financial circumstances, between the 4th and the 7th.

You need a deep commitment if you are to feel happy in your romantic associations this month. If you're in a new relationship, Mercury's association with Neptune in the zone of hidden secrets might cause you to doubt the integrity of the person with whom you are involved. Rumours and innuendos are not something you should pay too much attention to or you could completely bamboozle yourself. It's a time for trusting your heart and your insight into human nature, based on your own personal experience.

There's some good news for those of you in permanent relationships or a marriage because now Mars will move away from its difficult, challenging influence on Saturn, which recently has been affecting your domestic and personal relationships. This means an easing of tension, a higher quality of communication and a deeper trust and bonding between the two of you. In friendships, however, you may still be feeling a little angst and may have to confront people on issues that have been festering for some time. Be quietly assertive without losing your cool.

If some Arians have taken on a new role or career position recently, you might now find that 'the honeymoon is over' and you could be having misgivings about the changes you've made. But I say to you that you should persevere and not lose hope.

Of course, the first few months of any job require a great deal of adjustment and just now you might be feeling the heat. Take heart that, after the 26th, Jupiter will give you some inner promptings to lead you to believe the decision you've made was correct after all. Remain positive.

The period of the 27th to the 29th may be harrowing, with difficult aspects between Mercury, Saturn and the Sun. Analyse your subjects well before going to meetings and stick to the topic at hand. You can apply this principle to personal interactions as well. If you have any differences of opinion or disagreements, try not to dredge up the past. This will only make matters worse.

Romance and friendship

Desire could be an all-consuming fire for you this month, but what might seem worse is when your desires can't be fulfilled. As the month commences, the Moon transits from the 1st until the 3rd in the sign of Scorpio, then Sagittarius. This highlights your need for sexual and emotional satisfaction, but that may not be possible.

For some of you who have been single for a long while, the period of the 4th to the 12th inclusive might involve you looking more deeply at how you can satisfy yourself rather than demanding life brings you something that may not be your destiny. Remaining satisfied in yourself is a key component in attracting bigger and better things from the world around you.

There is a vast improvement for singles born under Aries after the 15th, with Venus entering into the seventh sign of marriage. This is truly an excellent period to seek out others of like-mind, and something interesting may cross your path when you least expect it. Uranus and Venus on the 17th bring surprises, excitement and a little bit of fear as well. You may not be prepared for someone you meet.

The new Moon on the 27th also picks up the pace for Aries, both singles and those otherwise committed, because this heralds the commencement of new love. There may also be some unexpected surprises offered to you by loved ones. A change of heart by someone in a relationship with you could also make you feel much more confident about your future prospects together.

Between the 25th and the 30th, Venus fast approaches the separative influence of Saturn in the romance area. A temporary separation may be necessary and completely out of your control. You should use this time to think about where you want to take your relationship and how you can improve yourself.

Work and money

With Venus and the Sun transiting your zone of work, you'll feel much lighter and happier about what you're doing in your current role.

You may not be feeling particularly energetic but you are able to be more creative and purposeful about where you're going. Take the time to plan and work behind the scenes. Connect with those who can make your dreams a reality. Particularly between the 1st and the 6th, you have the full support of your co-workers and staff if you're in a position of authority.

The 12th to the 15th is a period of travel and change. Don't postpone necessary journeys to tie up loose ends in business matters.

Contracts are slow, deliberate, but positive after the 23rd. Don't let hiccups on the 25th create doubt.

Sign off on paperwork on the 26th before Mercury creates havoc on the 27th. At least, if you've got the deal in the bag, you'll be able to sleep soundly.

Destiny dates

Positive: 1, 2, 3, 13, 14, 15, 23

Negative: None

Mixed: 4, 5, 6, 7, 8, 9, 10, 11, 12, 25, 26, 27, 28, 29, 30

OCTOBER 2011

Highlights of the month

Travel is on your mind and you'll feel restless throughout October. You're emotionally drawn to change, excitement and the spirit of adventure. Your mind is not on your work; Mercury in hard aspect to your career zone is testimony to that fact.

Between the 1st and the 4th you are somewhat scattered, so perhaps this is an ideal time to factor in some time out. Even if it's not a long holiday, consider a vacation to an interesting country. The point I'm making is that you may not feel settled enough to focus on your work and therefore the results if you do stay will be less than favourable. Get out and go with the flow of this energy.

An interesting phenomenon takes place for Aries in that four planets occupy the seventh zone of relationships in the moveable sign of Libra as October commences. It's not a well-known fact with western astrologers that the seventh house also deals with change, travel and, in some cases, especially due to Saturn's presence there, the relocation of one's domestic life and premises. For this reason I'm saying that some of you may seriously contemplate leaving your home, selling up and moving somewhere completely different.

You mustn't act upon a whim, however, and I suggest you think this through carefully. The likely time frame for this to happen would be when Mercury conjoins Saturn after the 7th, making you able to consider these issues slowly and deliberately. After the 10th, when Mercury posits your zone of shared resources, these influences may extend to talking to bank managers, insurance agents and others associated with the buying and selling of real estate.

Taxes, annuities and other loans or debts may need to be addressed during the second- and third-week period of October.

Sex is uppermost in your mind after the 18th, when the Sun enters your eighth zone of deep transformation, sexuality and intimacy. This is a time when you'll want to express these deeper, primal urges and demand that your partner does the same. However, if you happen to be out of sync with your spouse or lover, your desires may cause problems and could highlight the significant differences in your development. Talk through this with them, and then talk through it a little more.

You are wasteful with your ideas with Mercury opposing Jupiter, and possibly even wasteful with your money as well. Try to be frugal and of course consider the environment and other methods of saving energy. Contribute to the global effort to 'green the world'.

You are vital between the 20th and the 29th, with Mars causing you to be more physical. You'll actively participate in outdoor sports and other competitive activities. After the 30th is a good time to sign up to that gym membership you've been considering. If you've been feeling lazy, then at least putting your money where your mouth is will more than likely help you stick to a routine where you can improve your health, vitality and physical appearance as well.

Romance and friendship

You mustn't be too self-absorbed between the 1st and the 4th. Some of your friends might think this is a campaign to pull away from them when in fact you're preoccupied with your own personal problems. If you're with others during this period, try to put your issues aside for the time being and enjoy the company of those who care about you.

The full Moon of the 10th could make you overly reactive, so I'd suggest that you try waving your complaint at the appropriate person. It's times like these when you may take out your ill feelings on the wrong person.

It's not always a good policy to side with the minority just because you feel sorry for them. This will definitely be inappropriate behaviour between the 19th and the 23rd. Stay out of any controversy where people are trying to dump their emotional baggage on you. Don't get caught up in the crossfire; you might be seen as a do-gooder sitting on the wrong side.

Offering a deserving remark around the 26th could spark a new friendship that has long-term ramifications for you. The treasure of friendship—better still, of deep love and affection—is rare and here you perhaps have an opportunity to meet your soulmate.

After the 28th, you can't help condemning chocolate for being totally delicious and completely irresistible. At this time you have full permission to take a break out of your self-disciplined cycle of exercise and dieting to enjoy some of the finer things—that is, food—in life.

Work and money

There are some dicey work days for you in the early part of October, including the 1st, 3rd, 6th and the 11th. The word 'exploitation' could be ringing in your brain as you try to figure out whether or not others are simply taking advantage of you.

After the 12th, when the full Moon occurs in Aries, you will have a better handle on things, will understand clearly what the circumstances are and therefore will better know how to proceed.

If by the 22nd you're still not satisfied with what you observe, show your hand and demand your rights, particularly if this relates to money that you've been short-changed.

The new Moon on the 26th is excellent for sorting out your taxation, investments and other accounting issues. If you've been remiss in paying your tax, now is the time to get cracking so that you don't find yourself in hot water with the tax department.

Legal matters and contracts are also highlighted between the 29th and 31st. Don't be afraid to pay a professional appropriately for good advice.

Destiny dates

Positive: 12, 24, 25, 26, 27, 28

Negative: 6, 11, 19, 23

Mixed: 1, 2, 3, 4, 7, 10, 18, 20, 21, 22, 29, 30, 31

NOVEMBER 2011

Highlights of the month

This is a vital month for Aries, or should I say a vital period in your life, with the electric planet Uranus now in your Sun sign. This means you'll be keen to do things differently, to progress and gain recognition in different ways from the past.

However, this is a double-edged sword because, while you may be keen to exhibit the more unconventional aspects of your nature, doing so may not sit well with friends, co-workers and even family members who are more conservative and prefer to see you stay the same. Delicately balancing these two extremes will be a creative challenge for you.

Love, your social life and personal relationships are vastly improved after the 10th, with Venus moving out of the intense eighth zone of your horoscope to the ninth zone, which broadens your horizons and makes you feel much better.

Also with Mars, the passionate planet, in your fifth zone of love affairs at the same time, it's likely you'll want to express some of your more lustful desires, so hopefully you have someone with whom to share these passions. If you don't, you'll need some sort of alternative creative or physical outlet to do so in an acceptable manner.

Saturn will be edging towards the eighth zone after the 14th and therefore issues of mortality, philosophical and spiritual ideals will all come under the microscope for deeper scrutiny. You have an increased clarity and a focused level of concentration, which help you to solve deep and probing questions.

Some of these issues may centre around older members of the family, which is why you'll be drawn towards contemplating the future in a more practical way. Combining real day-to-day life issues with philosophical and abstract ideas requires a stroke of genius in a way, but at this time you're able to do it, and do it in a way that serves you and others well.

Serving others may not be easy, even though you have the desire to do so, particularly when the Sun and Neptune are in hard aspect after the 21st. You need to use some of your charm and persuasiveness to delegate some difficult and not-so-pleasant chores to others, either in the family or on the work front. This will give you the opportunity to focus on service and this practical spirituality that I'm talking about.

An important solar eclipse takes place on the 25th, again in your zone of self-transformation and sexuality. These issues that relate to the sign of Scorpio will be very powerful forces moulding and shaping your destiny during the coming months.

Be open to what is revealed within yourself, and don't necessarily feel as if you have to share these gems of wisdom with others. These are perhaps 'cosmic flashes', which are meant only for you, for your own personal evolution, at this time.

Romance and friendship

Good company, interesting e-mails, unconventional activities and generally good fun can be anticipated between the 2nd and the 5th. You can sense that routine affairs are killing your spontaneity and creativity, so this is the perfect time to try something out of the ordinary and to do it with others who are a little more bold and adventurous, just like you.

Uncalled-for advice on the 7th is not necessarily pleasant to hear but is probably right on the money. You'd be advised to take note of what is said and utilise it, even if you don't openly agree that the advice is correct.

Avoid trying a makeover on your partner between the 11th and the 14th. You must understand that, even if you're not satisfied with some of their habits, change has to come from within. Imposing your will on someone else now will only cause World War Three.

You could feel a little confused about your identity between the 21st and the 25th, on which date a solar eclipse takes place. Your ethics, your concept of how you should do things and how people perceive you, could be issues that you'll be mulling over. As always, being yourself is the best policy.

A sudden, exciting affair of the heart around the 27th may not last long but will give you loads of satisfaction, nonetheless. As long as you're not expecting a long-term relationship, a fun night out will still afford you immense pleasure.

The latter part of November, in particular the last few days, is excellent for getting out the travel brochures, investigating unusual destinations for holidaying and dreaming of the future. Between the 28th and the 30th, you should hop on the Internet and see what destinations are available to you in the coming months.

Work and money

You might overestimate your capabilities this month and accept too many tasks into your in-tray. Between the 1st and the 7th, you'll be busy, but probably more than you have to be. Prioritise tasks and don't try to play the martyr just because you know you have more energy than others.

Don't let wasteful extravagances put you in a ditch after the 9th. It's best to wait until the full Moon of the 10th before committing yourself to big-ticket items that you can ill afford.

You can, however, utilise the positive vibrations of Mars and Jupiter at this time to invest in things that will, in the long term, give you a good return on your money. Wisely look at what stocks and other commodities will return a slow, steady profit to you.

Communication may not flow as easily as it normally does for you this month and, rather than risk losing clients, especially if you're in the business of selling, advertising or working in the public relations field, it's best to think through your words carefully and send your proposals via e-mail or post.

With Venus in triune aspect to Jupiter on the 28th, your finances should improve markedly.

Destiny dates

Positive: 10, 27, 28, 29, 30

Negative: 9

Mixed: 1, 2, 3, 4, 5, 6, 7, 11, 12, 13, 14, 21, 22, 23, 24, 25

DECEMBER 2011

Highlights of the month

As an astrologer, I always love it when I can predict 'prosperity', particularly at the end of the year. And this is precisely what I will be forecasting for Aries-born natives, due to their ruling planet Mars being in a highly favourable and energetic aspect to their career sector.

In December, Mars and the Sun produce a sequence of forces that bring you to a peak. Coupled with Venus also transiting your zone of career and success, this is a powerful time when you can achieve some rather significant benefits through your professional life.

These influences are extraordinarily palpable up to and including the 6th, when Mercury also joins the cosmic dance in your horoscope.

Does this mean that Arian folk not working in a professional arena can't experience and enjoy these energies? Absolutely not. Let me say that these vibrations affect the quality of your work, irrespective of the arena in life that you happen to be stationed. If you're a parent, a home-maker or even 'the little old lady next door', the influences will be felt and your calibre of work, your skill in dealing with your day-to-day situations, will be markedly improved.

The effects of the lunar eclipse and also some of the lunar movements throughout the last month of the year also point to some fairly significant developments in your work, particularly in the way you see yourself and the way you want to present yourself to the world. This is important because it sets the trend for the coming few years and means that you'll be working hard to improve your relationships on all fronts of life.

Due to your extra efforts and Venus moving through the eleventh zone after the 16th, together with the Sun at the pinnacle of your horoscope on the same day, success of some sort should be felt at this time leading up to Christmas.

With an added benefit of a triangular relationship between the Sun and Jupiter on the 23rd, I can easily predict a very satisfying and fun-filled Christmas for 2011.

Many of the planetary influences this year have shaped you in such a way to create a desire for more progressive achievements, a deeper understanding of your relationships and possible permanent changes in your residential and career lives. Maintaining your self-confidence and optimism, thanks to Jupiter, means that the close of 2011 should bring a big smile to your face and some added anticipation that your future will be even brighter still.

Romance and friendship

Togetherness versus independence could well be one of the key issues for you in relationships in the final month of 2011. Take some time off between the 1st and the 4th if you feel you need some of your own space. It will do your relationship the world of good.

You'll be feeling more loving and kind to your partner when the Moon transits Jupiter after the 7th. Also, the full Moon on the 10th in your communications sphere is excellent for bridging any gap between you and your partner. Remember, sometimes it's easier to stick with the tried and true, even if there are moments of boredom that you'd like to get rid of.

Get creative with your friends and lovers between the 14th and the 17th. Two heads are better than one and the moment you start creatively sharing your ideas, you'll find it will bring you together more closely than before.

You may also feel the inner child in you busting to break forth and this is the time to do that, in spite of what others may think.

The final new Moon of the year takes place in Sagittarius, the lucky zone of your horoscope. Christmas should be a time of great fortune, goodwill and increased social activity. The period of the 24th to the 27th indicates an increasingly hectic social agenda. But, by the same token, some of your acquaintances may be envious of your extensive network of relationships and could be more than demanding on your time. You'll need to be everything to everyone this Christmas.

Try to resolve any outstanding conflicts between the 29th and the 31st. This will set your mind at peace and make you feel much better about moving forward into the upcoming year, 2012.

This is a time of new beginnings, of creativity, so don't let others pigeonhole you. You are your own person and should be free to enjoy and indulge yourself in the ways that you choose.

Work and money

If you're reluctant to 'get with the program' at work, utilise modern technology and avail yourself of such things as the Internet, text messages and other fantastic time-saving devices. You've only got yourself to blame if this month you're overloaded with chores that could otherwise be fixed in a jiffy. From the 2nd, take a little time to investigate how you can streamline your communication and any tasks that seem to be ever-mounting.

Money is plentiful from the 7th. Try bargain shopping to maintain a strong bank balance. It will be easy for you to splurge, however, so try purchasing some of the lesser-known brands as gifts for those who aren't necessarily close to you. Stretch that dollar and do it cleverly so that you satisfy your duty of giving without breaking the budget.

If you still feel passionate about your work between the 17th and the 24th, then use this feeling as a barometer of staying true to the course and not shifting midstream. It's likely the energy and the drive that you contribute to your workplace and the people you work with will continue to support you in the coming year.

This is a dynamic period for you. The final new Moon of 2011 takes place in your zone of higher learning, education and broadening of one's horizons. For this reason, the close of 2011 will be clearly focused on how you can improve yourself and your work skills to position yourself for an even more successful coming twelve months.

Destiny dates

Positive: 1, 2, 3, 4, 6, 7, 8, 9, 10, 14, 15, 16, 17, 18, 19, 20, 21, 22, 23

Negative: 29, 30, 31

Mixed: 24, 25, 26, 27

ARIES

2011:
Astronumerology

If you don't like something, change it. If you can't change it, change your attitude. Don't complain.

—Maya Angelou

The power behind your name

It's hard to believe that your name resonates with a numerical vibration, but it's true! By simply adding the numbers of your name, you can see which planet rules you and what effects your name will have on your life and destiny. According to the ancient Chaldean system of numerology, each number is assigned a planetary energy. Take a look at the chart below to see how each alphabetical letter is connected to a planetary energy:

AIQJY	**=**	**1**	**Sun**
BKR	**=**	**2**	**Moon**
CGLS	**=**	**3**	**Jupiter**
DMT	**=**	**4**	**Uranus**
EHNX	**=**	**5**	**Mercury**
UVW	**=**	**6**	**Venus**
OZ	**=**	**7**	**Neptune**
FP	**=**	**8**	**Saturn**
—	**=**	**9**	**Mars**

The number 9 is not allotted a letter because it is considered 'unknowable'. Once the numbers have been added, establish which single planet rules your name and personal affairs. At this point the number 9 can be used for interpretation. Do you think it's unusual that many famous actors, writers and musicians have modified their names? This is to attract luck and good fortune, which can be made easier by using the energies of a friendlier planet. Try experimenting with the table and see how new names affect you. It's so much fun, and you may even attract greater love, wealth and worldly success!

Look at the following example to work out the power of your name. A person named Andrew Brown would calculate his ruling planet by correlating each letter to a number in the table, like this:

A	**N**	**D**	**R**	**E**	**W**	**B**	**R**	**O**	**W**	**N**
1	**5**	**4**	**2**	**5**	**6**	**2**	**2**	**7**	**6**	**5**

Now add the numbers like this:

1 + 5 + 4 + 2 + 5 + 6 + 2 + 2 + 7 + 6 + 5 = 45

Then add 4 + 5 = 9

The ruling number of Andrew Brown's name is 9, which is ruled by Mars (see how the 9 can now be used?). Now study the name–number table to reveal the power of your name. The numbers 4 and 5 will also play a secondary role in Andrew's character and destiny, so in this case you would also study the effects of Uranus (4) and Mercury (5).Name–number table

Your name-number	Ruling planet	Your name characteristics
1	**Sun**	Attractive personality. Magnetic charm. Superman-, superwoman-like vitality and physical energy. Incredibly active and gregarious. Enjoys outdoor activities and sports. Has friends and individuals in powerful positions. Good government connections. Intelligent, spectacular, flashy and successful. A loyal number for love and relationships.
2	**Moon**	Feminine and soft, emotional temperament. Fluctuating moods but intuitive, and possibly even clairvoyant abilities. Ingenious nature and kind-hearted expression of feelings. Loves family, mothering and home life. Night owl who probably needs more sleep. Success with the public and/or women generally.
3	**Jupiter**	Sociable, optimistic number with fortunate destiny. Attracts opportunities without too much effort. Great sense of timing. Religious or spiritual inclinations. Naturally drawn to investigate the meaning of life. Philosophical insight. Enjoys travel and to explore the world and different cultures.
4	**Uranus**	Volatile character with many peculiar aspects. Likes to experiment and test novel experiences. Forward thinking, with many extraordinary friends. Gets bored easily so needs plenty of inspiring activities. Pioneering, technological and creative. Wilful and obstinate at times. Unforeseen events in life may be positive or negative.

Your name-number	Ruling planet	Your name characteristics
5	Mercury	Sharp wit, quick thinking and with great powers of speech. Extremely active life. Always on the go, living on nervous energy. Youthful outlook and never grows old. Looks younger than actual age. Young friends and humorous disposition. Loves reading and writing. Great communicator.
6	Venus	Delightful and charming. Graceful and eye-catching personality who cherishes and nourishes friends. Very active social life. Musical or creative interests. Great moneymaking opportunities as well as numerous love affairs indicated. Career in the public eye is quite likely. Loves family but is often troubled over divided loyalties with friends.
7	Neptune	Intuitive, spiritual and self-sacrificing nature. Easily duped by those who need help. Loves to dream of life's possibilities. Has healing powers. Dreams are revealing and prophetic. Loves water and will have many journeys in life. Spiritual aspirations dominate worldly desires.
8	Saturn	Hard-working, ambitious person with slow yet certain achievements. Remarkable concentration and self-sacrifice for a chosen objective. Financially focused but generous when a person's trust is gained. Proficient in one's chosen field but is a hard taskmaster. Demands perfection and needs to relax and enjoy life.

Your name-number	Ruling planet	Your name characteristics
9	**Mars**	Extraordinary physical drive, desires and ambition. Sports and outdoor activities are major keys to health. Confrontational but likes to work and play really hard. Protects and defends family, friends and territory. Individual tastes in life but also self-absorbed. Needs to listen to others' advice to gain greater successes.

Your 2011 planetary ruler

Astrology and numerology are intimately connected. As already shown, each planet rules over a number between 1 and 9. Both your name *and* your birth date are governed by planetary energies.

Simply add the numbers of your birth date and the year in question to find out which planet will control the coming year for you. Here is an example:

If you were born on the 12th of November, add the numerals 1 and 2, for your day of birth, and 1 and 1, for your month of birth, to the year in question, in this case 2011, the current year, like this:

Add 1 + 2 + 1 + 1 + 2 + 0 + 1+ 1 = 9

The planet ruling your individual karma for 2011 will be Mars because this planet rules the number 9.

You can even take your ruling name-number, as shown previously, and add it to the year in question, to throw more light on your coming personal affairs, like this:

A N D R E W B R O W N = 9

Year coming = 2011

Add 9 + 2 + 0 + 1 + 1 = 13

Add 1 + 3 = 4

This is the ruling year number, using your name-number as a basis.

Therefore, study Uranus's (number 4) influence for 2011. Enjoy!

1 is the year of the Sun

Overview

The year 2011 is the commencement of a new cycle for you. Because the Sun rules the number 1, the dominant energy for you in the coming year is solar, which is also connected to the sign of Leo. Expect the coming year to be full of great accomplishments and a high reputation regarding new plans and projects. This is the turning of a new page in the book of your life.

You will experience an uplifting of your physical energies, which makes you ready to assume fresh responsibilities in a new nine-year cycle. Whatever you begin now will surely be successful.

Your physical vitality is strong and your health should improve. If you've been suffering physical ailments, this is the time to improve your physical wellbeing because recovery will be certain.

You're a magnetic person this year, so attracting people into your life won't be difficult. Expect a new circle of friends and possibly even new lovers coming into your life. Get ready to be invited to many parties and different engagements. However, don't go burning the midnight oil because this will overstretch your physical powers.

Don't be too cocky with friends or employers. Maintain some humility, which will make you even more popular throughout 2011.

Love and pleasure

Because this is the commencement of a new cycle, you'll be lucky in love. The Sun also has influence over children, so your family life will also entail more responsibility. Music, art and any other creative activities will be high on your agenda and may be the source of a new romance for you.

Work

Because you are so popular and powerful this year, you won't need to exert too much effort to attract luck, money and new windows of opportunity through your work and group activities. Changes that you make professionally now will pay off, particularly in the coming couple of years. Promotions are likely and don't be surprised to see some extra money coming your way as a pay rise.

Improving your luck

Because Leo and the number 1 are your rulers this year, you'll be especially lucky without too much effort. The months of July and August, being ruled by Leo, are very lucky for you. The 1st, 8th, 15th and 22nd hours of Sundays will be especially lucky. You may also find yourself meeting Leos and they may be able to contribute something to your good fortune throughout the coming year.

This year your lucky numbers are 1, 10, 19 and 28.

2 is the year of the Moon

Overview

The Moon represents emotional, nurturing, mothering and feminine aspects of our natures and 2011 will embody all of these traits in you, and more.

Groundbreaking opportunities in your relationships with family members can be expected. This will offer you immense satisfaction.

Your emotional and mental moods and habits should be examined. If you are reactive in your life, this year will be the perfect time to take greater control of yourself. The sign of Cancer, which is ruled by the Moon, is also very much linked to the number 2 and therefore people born under this sign may have an important role to play in your life.

Love and pleasure

Your home, family life and interpersonal relationships will be the main arenas of activity for you in 2011. You'll be able to take your relationships to a new level. If you haven't had the time to dedicate and devote yourself to the people you love, you can do so throughout the coming twelve months.

Thinking of moving? These lunar energies may cause you to change your residence or renovate your current home to make your living circumstances much more in tune with your mind and your heart.

Work

Working from home can be a great idea—or at least, spending more time alone to focus your attention on what you really want—will benefit you professionally. You need to control yourself and think carefully about how you are going to achieve your desired goals.

Women can be a source of opportunity for you and, if you're looking for a change in work, use your connections, especially feminine ones, to achieve success.

Improving your luck

The sign of Cancer being ruled by the Moon also has a connection with Mondays and therefore this will be one of your luckier days throughout 2011. The month of July is also one in which some of your dreams may come true. The 1st, 8th, 15th and 22nd hours on Mondays are successful times. Pay special attention to the new and full Moons in 2011.

The numbers 2, 11, 20, 29 and 38 are lucky for you.

3 is the year of Jupiter

Overview

Number 3 is one of the luckiest numbers, being ruled by Jupiter. Therefore, 2011 should be an exciting and expansive year for you. The planet Jupiter and the sign of Sagittarius will dominate the affairs of your life.

Under the number 3 you'll desire a richer, deeper and broader experience of life and as a result your horizons will also be much broader. You have the ability to gain money, to increase your popularity, and to have loads of fun.

Generosity is one of the key words of the number 3 and you're likely to help others fulfil their desires, too. There is an element of humanity and self-sacrifice indicated by this number and so the more spiritual and compassionate elements of your personality will bubble to the surface. You can improve yourself as a person generally, and this is also a year when your good karma should be used unselfishly to help others as well as yourself.

Love and pleasure

Exploring the world through travel will be an important component of your social and romantic life throughout 2011. It's quite likely that, through your travels and your contacts in other places, you may meet people who will spur you on to love and romance.

You'll be a bit of a gambler in 2011 and the number 3 will make you speculative. This could mean a few false starts in the area of love, but don't be afraid to explore the signs of human possibilities. You may just meet your soulmate as a result.

If you're currently in a relationship, you can deepen your love for each other and push the relationship to new heights.

Work

This is a fortunate year for you. The year 2011 brings you opportunities and success. Your employers will listen to your ideas and accommodate your requests for extra money.

Starting a new job is likely, possibly even your own business. You will try something big and bold. Have no fear: success is on your side.

Improving your luck

As long as you don't push yourself too hard you will have a successful year. Maintain a first-class plan and stick to it. Be realistic about what you are capable of. On the 1st, 8th, 15th and 24th hours of Thursdays, your intuition will make you lucky.

Your lucky numbers this year are 3, 12, 21 and 30. March and December are lucky months. The year 2011 will bring you some unexpected surprises.

4 is the year of Uranus

Overview

Expect the unexpected in 2011. This is a year when you achieve extraordinary things but have to make serious choices between several opportunities. You need to break free of your own past self-limitations, off-load any baggage that is hindering you, in both your personal and professional lives. It's an independent year and self-development will be important to achieving success.

Discipline is one of your key words for 2011. Maintain an orderly lifestyle, a clear-cut routine, and get more sleep. You'll gain strong momentum to fulfil yourself in each and every department of your life.

Love and pleasure

You may be dissatisfied with the current status quo in your relationships, so you're likely to break free and experiment with something different. Your relationships will be anything but dull or routine. You're looking for someone who is prepared to explore emotional and sexual landscapes.

Your social life will also be exciting and you'll meet unusual people who will open your eyes to new and fruitful activities. Spiritual and self-help activities will also capture your attention and enable you to make the most of your new friendships.

Work

The number 4 is modern, progressive and ruled by Uranus. Due to this, all sorts of technological gadgets, computing and Internet activities will play a significant role in your professional life. Move ahead with the times and upgrade your professional skills, because any new job you attempt will require it.

Work could be a little overwhelming, especially if you've not been accustomed to keeping a tight schedule. Be more efficient with your time.

Groups are important to your work efforts this year, so utilise your friends in finding a position you desire. Listen to their advice and become more of a team player because this will be a short cut in your pathway to success.

Improving your luck

Slow your pace this year because being impulsive will only cause you to make errors and waste time. 'Patience is a virtue', but in your case, when being ruled by the number 4, patience will be even more important for you.

The 1st, 8th, 15th and 20th hours of any Saturday will be very lucky for you in 2011.

Your lucky numbers are 4, 13, 22 and 31.

5 is the year of Mercury

Overview

Owing to the rulership of 2011 by the number 5, your intellectual and communicative abilities will be at a peak. Your imagination is also greatly stimulated by Mercury and so exciting new ideas will be constantly churning in your mind.

The downside of the number 5 is its convertible nature, which means it's likely that, when crunch times come and you have to make decisions, it will be difficult to do so. Get all your information together before drawing a firm conclusion. Develop a strong will and unshakable attitude to overcome distractions.

Contracts, new job offers and other agreements also need to be studied carefully before coming to any decision. Business skills and communication are the key words for your life in 2011.

Love and pleasure

One of the contributing factors to your love life in 2011 is service. You must learn to give to your partner if you wish to receive. There may be a change in your routine and this will be necessary if you are to keep your love life exciting, fresh and alive.

You could be critical, so be careful if you are trying to correct the behaviour of others. You'll be blunt and this will alienate you from your peers. Maintain some control over your critical mind before handing out your opinions.

You are likely to become interested in beautifying yourself and looking your best.

Work

Your ideas will be at the forefront of your professional activities this year. You are fast, capable and also innovative in the way you conduct yourself in the workplace. If you need to make any serious changes, however, it is best to think twice before 'jumping out of the pan and into the fire'.

Travel will also be a big component of your working life this year, and you can expect a hectic schedule with lots of flitting about here, there and everywhere. Pace yourself.

Improving your luck

Your greatest fortune will be in communicating ideas. Don't jump from one idea to another too quickly, though, because this will dilute your success.

Listen to your body signals as well because your health is strongly governed by the number 5. Sleep well, eat sensibly and exercise regularly to rebuild your resilience and strength.

The 1st, 8th, 15th and 20th hours of Wednesdays are your luckiest, so schedule your meetings and other important social engagements at these times.

Throughout 2011 your lucky numbers are 5, 14, 23 and 32.

6 is the year of Venus

Overview

The number 6 can be summed up in one beautiful four-letter word: LOVE! Venus rules 6 and is well known for its sensual, romantic and marital overtones. The year 2011 offers you all of this and more. If you're looking for a soulmate, it's likely to happen under a 6 vibration.

This year is a period of hard work to improve your security and finances. Saving money, cutting costs and looking to your future will be important. Keep in mind that this is a year of sharing love *and* material resources.

Love and pleasure

Romance is a key feature of 2011 and, if you're currently in a relationship, you can expect it to become more fulfilling. Important karmic connections are likely during this 6 year for those of you who are not yet married or in a relationship.

Beautify yourself, get a new hairstyle, work on looking your best through improving your fashion sense, new styles of jewellery and getting out there and showing the world what you're made of. This is a year in which your social engagements result in better relationships.

Try not to overdo it, because Venus has a tendency towards excess. Moderation in all things is important in a Venus year 6.

Work

The year 2011 will stimulate your knowledge about finance and your future security. You'll be capable of cutting back expenses and learning how to stretch a dollar. There could be surplus cash this year, increased income or some additional bonuses. You'll use this money to improve your living circumstances because home life is also important under a 6 year.

Your domestic situation could also be tied in with your work. During this year of Venus, your business and social activities will overlap.

Improving your luck

Money will flow as long as you keep an open mind and positive attitude. Remove negative personality traits obstructing you from greater luck. Be moderate in your actions and don't focus primarily on money. Your spiritual needs also require attention.

The 1st, 8th, 15th and 20th hours on Fridays are extremely lucky for you this year and new opportunities can arise when you least expect it.

The numbers 6, 15, 24 and 33 will generally increase your luck.

7 is the year of Neptune

Overview

Under a 7 year of Neptune, your spiritual and intuitive powers peak. Although your ideals seem clearer and more spiritually orientated, others may not understand your purpose. Develop the power of your convictions to balance your inner ideals with the practical demands of life.

You must learn to let go of your past emotional issues, break through these barriers to improve your life and your relationships this year. This might require you to sever ties with some of the usual people you have become accustomed to being with, which will give you the chance to focus on your own inner needs.

Love and pleasure

Relationships may be demanding and it's at this point in your life that you'll realise you have to give something to yourself as well, not just give to others indefinitely. If the people that matter most in your life are not reciprocating and meeting your needs, you'll have to make some important changes this year.

When it comes to helping others, pick your mark. Not everyone is deserving of the love and resources you have to offer. If you're indiscriminate, you could find yourself with egg on your face if you have been taken advantage of. Be firm, but compassionate.

Work

Compassionate work best describes 2011 under a 7 year. But the challenges of your professional life give you greater insight into yourself and the ability to see clearly what you *don't* want in your life any more. Remove what is unnecessary and this will pave the way for brighter successes.

Caring for and helping others will be important because your work will now bring you to a point where you realise that selfishness, money and security are not the only important things in life. Helping others will be part of your process, which will bring excellent benefits.

Improving your luck

Self-sacrifice, along with discipline and personal discrimination, bring luck. Don't let people use you because this will only result in more emotional baggage. The law of karma states that what you give, you will receive in greater measure; but sometimes the more you give, the more people take, too. Remember that.

The 1st, 8th, 15th and 20th hours of Tuesdays will be lucky times this year.

Try the numbers 7, 16, 25 and 34 to increase your luck.

8 is the year of Saturn

Overview

The number 8 is the most practical of the numbers, being ruled by Saturn and Capricorn. This means that your discipline, attention to detail and hard work will help you achieve your goals. Remaining solitary and not being overly involved with people will help you focus on things that matter. Resisting temptation will be part of your challenge this year, but doing so will also help you become a better person.

Love and pleasure

Balance your personal affairs with work. If you pay too much attention to your work, finances and your professional esteem, you may be missing out on the simple things in life, mainly love and affection.

Being responsible is certainly a great way to show your love to the ones who matter to you, such as your family members. But if you're concerned only with work and no play, it makes for a very dull family life. Make a little more time to enjoy your family and friends and schedule some time off on the weekends so you can enjoy the journey, not just the goal.

Work

You can make a lot of money this year and, if you've been focused on your work for the last couple of years, this is a time when money should flow to you. The Chinese believe the number 8 is indeed the money number and can bring you the fruits of your hard labour.

Because you're cautious and resourceful you'll be able to save more this year, but try not to be too stingy with your money.

Under an 8 year you'll take on new responsibilities. You mustn't do this for the sake of looking good. If you truly like the work that is being offered, by all means take it. But if it's simply for the sake of ego, you'll be very disappointed.

Improving your luck

This year you could be a little reluctant to try new things. But if you are overly cautious, you may miss opportunities. Don't act impulsively on what is being offered, of course, but do be open to trying some alternative things as well.

Be gentle and kind to yourself. By pampering yourself you send out a strong signal to the universe that you are deserving of some rewards.

The 1st, 8th, 15th and 20th hours of Saturdays are the best times for you in 2011.

The numbers 1, 8, 17, 26 and 35 are your lucky numbers.

9 is the year of Mars

Overview

The year 2011 is the final year of a nine-year cycle and this will be dominated by Aries and Mars. You'll be rushing madly to complete many things, so be careful not to overstep the mark of your capability. Work hard but balance your life with adequate rest.

In your relationships you will realise that you are at odds with your partner and want different things. This is the time to talk it out. If the communication between you isn't flowing well, you might find yourself leaving the relationship and moving on to bigger or better things. Worthwhile communication is a two-way street that will benefit both of you.

Love and pleasure

Mars is very pushy and infuses the number 9 with this kind of energy. The upshot is you need to be gentle in conveying your ideas and offering your views. Avoid arguments if you want to improve your relationships.

If you feel it's time for a change, discuss it with your partner. You can work through this feeling together and create an exciting new pathway for your love life. Don't get too angry with the little things in life. Get out and play some sport if you feel you are inappropriately taking out your bad moods on the ones you love.

Work

You have an intense drive and strong capability to achieve anything you choose in 2011. But be careful you don't overdo things, because you are prone to pushing yourself too far. Pace your deadlines, stagger the workload and, if possible, delegate some of the more menial tasks to others so you'll have time to do your own work properly.

Number 9 has an element of leadership associated with it, so you may be asked to take over and lead the group. This brings with it added responsibility but can also inspire you greatly.

Improving your luck

Restlessness is one of the problems that the number 9 brings with it, so you must learn to meditate and pacify your mind so you can take advantage of what the universe has to offer. If you're scattered in your energies, your attention will miss vital opportunities and your relationships could also become rather problematic as well.

Your health and vitality will remain strong as long as you rest adequately and find suitable outlets for your tension.

The 1st, 8th, 15th and 20th hours of Tuesdays will be lucky for you throughout 2011. Your lucky numbers are 9, 18, 27 and 36.

ARIES

2011:
Your Daily Planner

Folks who never do any more than they are paid for,
never get paid more than they do.

—Elbert Hubbard

There is a little-known branch of astrology called electional astrology, and it can help you select the most appropriate times for many of your day-to-day activities.

Ancient astrologers understood the planetary patterns and how they impacted on each of us. This allowed them to suggest the best possible times to start various important activities. Many farmers today still use this approach: they understand the phases of the Moon, and attest to the fact that planting seeds on certain lunar days produces a far better crop than planting on other days.

The following section covers many areas of day-to-day life, and uses the cycles of the Moon and the combined strength of the other planets to work out the best times to start different types of activity.

So to create your own personal almanac, first select the activity you are interested in, then quickly scan the year for the best months to start it. When you have selected the month, you can finetune your timing by finding the best specific dates. You can then be sure that the planetary energies will be in sync with you, offering you the best possible outcome.

Coupled with what you know about your monthly and weekly trends, the daily planner can be a powerful tool to help you capitalise on opportunities that come your way this year.

Good luck, and may the planets bless you with great success, fortune and happiness in 2011!

Starting activities

How many times have you made a new year's resolution to begin a diet or be a better person in your relationships? And how many times has it not worked out? Well, part of the reason may be that you started out at the wrong time, because how successful you are is strongly influenced by the position of the Moon and the planets when you begin a particular activity. You will be more successful with the following endeavours if you start them on the days indicated.

Relationships

We all feel more empowered on some days than on others. This is because the planets have some power over us—their movement and their relationships to each other determine the ebb and flow of our energies. And our level of self-confidence and our sense of romantic magnetism play an important part in the way we behave in relationships.

Your daily planner tells you the ideal dates for meeting new friends, initiating a love affair, spending time with family and loved ones—it even tells you the most appropriate times for sexual encounters.

You'll be surprised at how much more impact you can make in your relationships when you tune yourself in to the planetary energies on these special dates.

Falling in love or restoring love

During these times you could expect favourable energies to be present to meet your soulmate. Or, if you've had difficulty in a relationship, you can approach the one you love to rekindle both your and their emotional responses.

January	8, 9, 10, 13, 14, 15, 18, 19, 20, 21
February	4, 5, 6, 9, 10, 11, 14
March	1, 9, 10, 14, 15, 16, 17
April	5, 6, 17, 25, 26
May	3, 4, 6, 7, 8, 9, 10, 11, 14, 15, 22, 23, 24
June	1, 11, 18, 19, 20, 28, 29, 30
July	7, 8, 26, 27, 30, 31
August	3, 12, 13, 14, 22, 23, 27, 31
September	1, 18, 19, 20, 26, 27, 28, 29, 30
October	12, 13, 17, 18, 25, 26, 29, 30, 31
November	2, 3, 4, 5, 6, 9, 17, 29
December	3, 7, 8, 11, 14, 15, 18, 19, 29, 30

Special times with friends and family

Socialising, partying and having a good time with those you enjoy being with is highly favourable under the following dates. These are also excellent days to spend time with family and loved ones in a domestic environment:

January	17, 20, 21
February	2, 9, 10, 11, 18, 19, 20, 21, 22, 23, 24, 28
March	1, 11, 14, 16, 17, 20
April	2, 11, 12, 21, 22, 26
May	6, 9, 10, 11, 14, 15, 22, 23, 24
June	4, 8, 10, 12, 19, 20, 25, 26, 28
July	7, 8, 16, 23, 30, 31
August	4, 5, 6, 7, 13, 20, 27, 31
September	1, 6, 18, 19, 20, 29, 30
October	1, 16, 17, 25, 26
November	2, 12, 13, 17, 26, 29
December	11, 14, 15, 18, 19, 27, 28

Healing or resuming a relationship

If you're trying to get back together with the one you love and need a heart-to-heart or deep and meaningful conversation, you can try the following dates to do so:

January	2, 3, 4, 5, 6, 7, 8, 9, 10, 11, 12, 13, 14, 15, 16, 17, 18, 19, 20, 21, 28
February	1, 2, 4, 5, 6, 7, 21, 22, 23, 24, 28
March	1, 8, 9, 10, 11, 14, 16, 17, 18, 19, 20

April	2, 11, 12, 26
May	1, 6, 7, 8, 9, 10, 11, 12, 13, 15, 19, 22, 24, 25, 26, 27, 28
June	5, 12, 14, 15, 16, 19, 23, 25, 26, 27, 28, 29, 30
July	4, 6, 7, 8, 9, 10, 16, 19, 21, 23, 28, 29, 30, 31
August	1, 2, 3, 13, 15, 16, 20, 27, 29, 30, 31
September	1, 2, 3, 4, 5, 6, 13, 15, 16, 17, 18, 19, 20, 21, 22, 23, 25, 28, 29
October	12, 13, 15, 16, 17, 18, 25, 27, 29
November	2, 4, 5, 6, 15, 16, 17, 26, 29
December	11, 19, 20, 21, 22, 23

Sexual encounters

Physical and sexual energies are well favoured on the following dates. The energies of the planets enhance your moments of intimacy during these times:

January	2, 3, 4, 5, 6, 7, 8, 9, 10, 11, 12, 20, 21, 25
February	7, 8, 18, 19, 20, 21
March	1, 8, 11, 14, 20, 21
April	4, 11, 12, 25, 26, 27, 28, 29
May	2, 9, 10, 11, 14, 15, 22, 23, 24
June	1, 11, 12, 18, 19, 20, 28, 29, 30

July	7, 8, 16, 19, 20, 21, 23, 30
August	3, 12, 13, 14, 20, 22, 27, 31
September	1, 18, 19, 20, 29, 30
October	1, 13, 15, 18, 19, 20, 21, 22, 25, 26
November	2, 3, 11, 15, 16, 17, 18, 21, 22
December	5, 6, 12, 13, 14, 15, 18, 19

Health and wellbeing

Your aura and life force are susceptible to the movements of the planets; in particular, they respond to the phases of the Moon.

The following dates are the most appropriate times to begin a diet, have cosmetic surgery, or seek medical advice. They also tell you when the best times are to help others.

Feeling of wellbeing

Your physical as well as your mental alertness should be strong on these following dates. You can plan your activities and expect a good response from others:

January	7, 9, 10, 11, 12, 13, 14, 18, 20, 21
February	4, 18, 19, 20, 21, 22, 23, 24
March	16, 17, 19, 20
April	2, 7, 12, 20, 22, 25, 26
May	9, 10, 11, 14, 15, 16, 17, 22, 24, 25

June	4, 8, 10, 11, 12, 16, 17, 18, 19, 20, 21, 23, 25, 26
July	7, 8, 9, 10, 26, 27, 30
August	3, 4, 5, 6, 12, 13, 14, 17, 19, 22, 27, 31
September	1, 13, 26, 27, 28, 29, 30
October	1, 16, 17, 25, 26, 30, 31
November	1, 2, 3, 4, 5, 6, 17, 29
December	4, 11, 14, 15, 18, 19, 21, 22, 23, 30

Healing and medical

These times are good for approaching others who have expertise when you need some deeper understanding. They are also favourable for any sort of healing or medication, and for making appointments with doctors or psychologists. Planning surgery around these dates should bring good results.

Often giving up our time and energy to assist others doesn't necessarily result in the expected outcome. By lending a helping hand to a friend on the following dates, the results should be favourable:

January	1, 2, 3, 4, 5, 6, 7, 8, 14, 15, 16, 17, 18, 19, 20, 21, 22, 23, 24, 25, 26, 27, 28, 29, 31
February	3, 4, 5, 6, 7, 8, 9, 10, 13, 15, 16, 17, 18, 19, 21, 22, 23, 24, 25, 26, 27
March	4, 9, 10, 11, 12, 15, 16

April	2, 9, 10, 11, 12, 13, 14, 15, 16, 17, 18, 19, 20, 21, 22, 23, 24, 25, 26, 27, 28, 29, 30
May	1, 2, 3, 4, 5, 6, 8, 9, 10, 11, 12, 13, 14, 15, 16, 17, 18, 19, 20, 21, 22, 23, 24, 25, 30
June	23, 26, 28
July	3, 10, 11, 12
August	7, 8, 9, 10, 11, 12, 13, 14, 15, 16, 20, 21, 25
September	23, 25, 26, 27
October	20, 21, 22, 23, 24, 25, 26, 27, 28, 29, 30, 31
November	1, 2, 3, 4, 5, 6, 7, 8, 9, 10, 11, 12, 13, 14, 15, 16, 17, 18, 19, 20, 21, 22, 23, 24, 25, 30
December	1, 2, 3, 4, 5, 6, 7, 8, 9, 10, 30

Money

Money is an important part of life, and involves lots of decisions—decisions about borrowing, investing, spending. The ideal times for transactions are very much influenced by the planets, and whether your investment or nest egg grows or doesn't grow can often be linked to timing. Making your decisions on the following dates could give you a whole new perspective on your financial future:

Managing wealth and money

To build your nest egg it's a good time to open a bank account and invest money on the following dates:

January	2, 3, 9, 10, 11, 12, 13, 14, 15, 16, 17, 18, 19, 20, 21, 22, 24, 28
February	3, 4, 5, 6, 7, 8, 9, 11, 13, 14, 16, 18, 19, 20, 21, 22, 23, 24, 25, 26, 27
March	4, 8, 11, 12, 13, 14, 16, 17, 18, 19
April	2, 7, 8, 9, 10, 11, 12, 13, 16, 17, 18, 19, 20, 21, 22, 23, 24, 25
May	1, 6, 7, 8, 9, 10, 11, 12, 13, 14, 15, 16, 17, 18, 19, 20, 21, 22, 23, 24, 25, 30
June	3, 4, 5, 8, 16, 17, 18, 19, 20, 23, 25, 26, 27, 28
July	4, 5, 6, 7, 8, 9, 10, 11, 12, 16, 23, 25, 28, 29, 30, 31
August	1, 2, 3, 4, 5, 6, 7, 8, 9, 10, 11, 12, 13, 14, 15, 16, 17, 19, 20, 30, 31
September	2, 11, 13, 15, 23, 25, 26, 27, 28, 29, 30
October	1, 2, 3, 4, 5, 6, 7, 8, 13, 14, 15, 16, 17, 18, 19, 21, 24, 25, 26, 27, 28, 29, 30, 31
November	2, 3, 4, 5, 6, 7, 9, 11, 12, 13, 14, 15, 16, 17, 18, 19, 20, 23, 25, 29
December	6, 13, 19, 26, 31

Spending

It's always fun to spend, but the following dates are more in tune with this activity and are likely to give you better results:

January	8, 9, 10, 11, 12, 13, 14, 15
February	9, 11, 18, 19
March	9
April	22
May	6, 7, 8, 9, 10, 11, 12, 13, 14, 17, 18, 19, 20, 21, 22, 23, 24
June	4, 8, 10, 11, 12, 14, 16, 17, 19
July	6, 7, 8, 9, 10, 11, 31
August	1, 2, 3, 4, 5, 6, 15, 16, 17, 18, 19, 30, 31
September	1, 2, 3, 4, 17, 19, 28, 29, 30
October	12, 13, 14, 15, 16, 17, 18, 19, 27, 28, 29, 30, 31
November	2, 3, 4, 5, 6, 7
December	3, 4, 5, 22, 23

Selling

If you're thinking of selling something, whether it is small or large, consider the following dates as ideal times to do so:

January	2, 3, 9, 10, 11, 12, 13, 14, 15, 16, 17, 18, 19, 20, 22, 24, 28
February	3, 4, 5, 6, 7, 8, 9, 11, 13, 14, 16, 18, 19, 20, 21, 22, 23, 24, 25, 26, 27
March	4, 8, 11, 12, 13, 14, 16, 17, 18, 19
April	2, 7, 8, 9, 10, 11, 12, 13, 16, 17, 18, 19, 20, 21, 22, 23, 24
May	1, 6, 7, 8, 9, 10, 11, 12, 13, 14, 15, 16, 17, 18, 19, 20, 21, 22, 23, 24, 25, 26, 30
June	3, 4, 5, 8, 16, 17, 18, 19, 20, 23, 25, 26, 27, 28
July	4, 5, 6, 7, 8, 9, 10, 11, 12, 16, 23, 25, 28, 29, 30, 31
August	1, 2, 3, 4, 5, 6, 7, 8, 9, 10, 11, 12, 13, 14, 15, 16, 17, 19, 20, 30, 31
September	2, 11, 13, 15, 23, 25, 26, 27, 28, 29, 30
October	1, 2, 3, 4, 5, 6, 7, 8, 13, 14, 15, 16, 17, 18, 19, 21, 24, 25, 26, 27, 28, 29, 30, 31
November	2, 3, 4, 5, 6, 7, 9, 11, 12, 13, 14, 15, 16, 17, 18, 19, 20, 23, 25, 29
December	2, 3, 4, 5, 6, 7, 11, 30

Borrowing

Few of us like to borrow money, but if you must, taking out a loan on the following dates will be positive:

January	1, 20, 21, 26, 27, 28, 31
February	1, 2, 22, 23, 24
March	1, 22, 23, 26, 27, 29, 31
April	1, 18, 19, 22, 23, 24, 25, 26, 27, 28, 29
May	17, 18, 19, 20, 21, 22, 23, 24, 25, 26
June	16, 17, 18, 19, 22
July	15, 16, 28, 29, 30
August	15, 16, 24, 25, 26, 27, 28
September	21, 22
October	21
November	14, 15, 16, 17, 23, 24
December	12, 13, 14, 15, 20, 21, 22, 23, 24

Speculation and investment

To invest your money and get a good return on that investment try taking a punt on the following dates:

January	3, 4, 5, 11, 12, 18, 19, 24, 25, 31
February	1, 7, 8, 14, 15, 20, 21, 27, 28
March	6, 7, 8, 14, 15, 20, 21, 26, 27
April	2, 3, 4, 10, 11, 16, 17, 22, 23, 24, 30
May	1, 7, 8, 14, 15, 20, 21, 27, 28, 29
June	3, 4, 5, 10, 11, 16, 17, 23, 24, 25
July	1, 2, 7, 8, 14, 15, 21, 22, 28, 29

August	3, 4, 10, 11, 17, 18, 19, 24, 25, 26, 31
September	1, 6, 7, 13, 14, 15, 21, 22, 27, 28
October	3, 4, 5, 11, 12, 18, 19, 25, 26, 31
November	1, 7, 8, 14, 15, 16, 21, 22, 27, 28
December	4, 5, 6, 12, 13, 18, 19, 25, 26, 31

Work and education

Your career is important to you, and continual improvement of your skills is therefore also crucial, professionally, mentally and socially. These dates will help you find out the most appropriate times to improve your professional talents and commence new work or education associated with your work.

You may need to decide when to start learning a new skill, when to ask for a promotion, and even when to make an important career change. Here are the days when your mental and educational power is strong.

Learning new skills

Educational pursuits are lucky and bring good results on the following dates:

January	16, 17
February	12, 13
March	11, 12, 13, 18, 19
April	7, 8, 9, 14, 15
May	5, 6, 12, 13

June	2, 8, 9, 14, 15
July	5, 6, 11, 12, 13
August	1, 2, 8, 9, 29, 30
September	4, 5
October	1, 2, 29, 30
November	25, 26
December	9, 10

Changing career path or profession

If you're feeling stuck and need to move into a new professional activity, changing jobs is recommended at these times:

January	4, 5, 13, 14, 15
February	9, 10, 11
March	1, 2, 3, 9, 10, 11, 12, 18, 19, 20, 21
April	5, 6, 7, 8, 9, 14, 15, 16, 17, 25, 26
May	3, 4, 12, 13, 22, 23, 24
June	1, 2, 8, 9, 18, 19, 20, 28, 29, 30
July	5, 6, 14, 26, 27
August	3, 4, 10, 11, 22, 23, 29, 30, 31
September	1, 6, 7, 8, 9, 10, 18, 19, 20, 27, 28
October	3, 4, 5, 16, 17, 25, 26, 31
November	1, 2, 3, 9, 10, 29, 30
December	1, 7, 8, 9, 10, 11, 18, 19, 25, 26, 27, 28

Promotion, professional focus and hard work

To increase your mental focus and achieve good results from the work you do; promotions are also likely on the dates that follow:

January	3, 9, 10, 11, 12, 13, 14, 18
February	22, 23, 24, 25, 26, 27, 28
March	8, 10, 11, 13, 14, 16, 17, 18, 19
April	11, 12
May	6, 7, 8, 9, 10, 11, 12, 13, 15, 16, 17, 19, 21, 22, 23, 24
June	4, 5, 8, 11, 12, 14, 15, 16, 17, 19
July	16, 18, 19, 20, 23, 24, 25, 28, 29, 30
August	1, 2, 14, 15, 16, 17, 19, 30
September	1, 2, 3, 4, 5, 6, 11, 13, 16, 17, 19
October	13, 15, 16, 17, 18, 19
November	2, 4, 5, 6, 7, 12
December	25, 26

Travel

Setting out on a holiday or adventurous journey is exciting. Here are the most favourable times for doing this. Travel on the following dates is likely to give you a sense of fulfilment:

January	9, 10, 11, 12, 16, 17, 18, 19
February	4, 5, 6, 7, 15

March	19
April	7, 8, 9, 10, 11
May	15
June	4, 8, 10, 11
July	1, 5, 6
August	1, 2, 3, 4, 8
September	27, 28
October	1, 3, 4, 29, 30, 31
November	1, 4, 5, 6
December	3, 4, 5, 25, 29, 30

Beauty and grooming

Believe it or not, cutting your hair or nails has a powerful effect on your body's electromagnetic energy. If you cut your hair or nails at the wrong time of the month, you can reduce your level of vitality significantly. Use these dates to ensure you optimise your energy levels by staying in tune with the stars:

Haircuts

January	1, 2, 8, 9, 10, 16, 17, 28, 29, 30
February	25, 26
March	4, 5, 11, 12, 13, 14, 25, 31
April	1, 7, 8, 9, 20, 21, 27, 28, 29
May	5, 6, 18, 19, 25, 26

June	1, 2, 14, 15, 21, 22, 28, 29, 30
July	11, 12, 13, 18, 19, 20, 26, 27
August	8, 9, 15, 16, 22, 23
September	4, 5, 11, 12, 18, 19, 20
October	1, 2, 8, 9, 10, 16, 17, 29, 30
November	4, 5, 6, 12, 13, 25, 26
December	2, 3, 9, 10, 11, 23, 24, 29, 30

Cutting nails

January	11, 12, 13, 14, 15, 18, 19, 20, 21
February	7, 8, 9, 10, 11, 14, 16
March	6, 8, 9, 10, 14, 15
April	2, 3, 5, 6
May	4, 7, 8, 9, 10, 11, 27, 28, 29, 30, 31
June	3, 4, 5, 6, 7, 23, 25, 26, 27
July	1, 2, 3, 21, 22, 23, 24, 25, 28, 29, 30, 31
August	17, 19, 20, 24, 25, 26
September	13, 16, 17, 21, 22, 23, 24
October	11, 13, 15, 18, 19, 20, 21, 22
November	15, 16, 17, 18
December	4, 5, 6, 7, 8

Therapies, massage and self-pampering

January	1, 2, 8, 9, 10, 16, 17, 28, 29, 30
February	5, 6, 12, 13, 25, 26
March	4, 5, 11, 12, 13, 24, 25, 31
April	1, 7, 8, 9, 20, 21, 27, 28, 29
May	5, 6, 18, 19, 25, 26
June	1, 2, 14, 15, 21, 22, 28, 29, 30
July	11, 12, 13, 18, 19, 20, 26, 27
August	8, 9, 15, 16, 22, 23
September	4, 5, 11, 12, 18, 19, 20
October	1, 2, 8, 9, 10, 16, 17, 29, 30
November	4, 5, 6, 12, 13, 25, 26
December	2, 3, 9, 10, 11, 23, 24, 29, 30